TERRORISM AND REAL

Selected Speeches of

DR MAHATHIR MOHAMAD

Prime Minister of Malaysia

Edited by

HASHIM MAKARUDDIN

Terrorism and the Real Issues
Selected Speeches of Dr Mahathir Mohamad
Prime Minister of Malaysia

Published by
Pelanduk Publications (M) Sdn Bhd
(Co. No. 113307-W)
12 Jalan SS13/3E, Subang Jaya Industrial Estate
47500 Subang Jaya, Selangor Darul Ehsan, Malaysia

for the
Prime Minister's Office of Malaysia
Putrajaya, Malaysia

Visit us at *www.pelanduk.com*
e-mail: *rusaone@tm.net.my*

Mahathir bin Mohamad, Dato' Seri, 1925-
Terrorism and the real issues / Mahathir Mohamad; edited by
Hashim Makaruddin.
ISBN 967-978-860-1
1. Terrorism—Religious aspects—Islam. 2. International offenses.
3. Islam and world politics. I. Hashim Makaruddin. II. Title.
303.625

Printed and bound in Malaysia

Contents

Foreword

"Dr Mahathir believes that the principal causes of terrorism need to be addressed urgently. He insists that unless these root causes are eliminated, the fight against terrorism will never succeed."

THE BURNING QUESTION of terrorism reemerged as an international problem in the aftermath of the September 11, 2001 tragedy. In this timely compilation of speeches, Dr Mahathir Mohamad addresses this issue from various perspectives, including its causes, dimension, impact and its remedy.

Dr Mahathir insists that a universal definition of terrorism should be properly formulated and accepted by all. He argues that terrorism should not be linked to any particular religion, race or creed. Linking Islam to terrorism is completely unjustified. Terrorism is not exclusively related to any religion. He fears that religious classification may lead to an indictment or a wholesale charge against Islam which will lead to unwarranted prejudice and hatred.

The terrorism that we see today is a by-product of the prolonged oppression and humiliation felt by a particular segment of the world's population against the perpetrators. Faced with terror attacks, they seek to redress the situation by resorting to attacks against the perpetrators. Dr Mahathir believes that the most effective way to combat terrorism apart from military action is to conduct a campaign to win the hearts and minds of those who sympathise with and support terrorists and even terrorists themselves.

Dr Mahathir believes that the principal causes of terrorism need to be addressed urgently. He insists that unless these root causes are eliminated, the fight against terrorism will never succeed. He makes frequent reference to the successful Malaysian experience in combating terrorism and offers to share this knowledge with the rest of the world.

The threat of terrorism is real and current. In the broader context of the subject, Dr Mahathir explains that terrorism is as globalised as trade and investment. He warns that the magnitude of the struggle to confront terrorism may escalate into "World War III". Such a war will be more complex in view of the nature of today's terrorism which transcends all borders and boundaries. Without any territorial limit, the problem can become extremely difficult to handle.

Dr Mahathir warns of another type of terrorism—economic terrorism. While physical militant attacks terrify their potential victims, economic actions such as sanctions and currency manipulation terrify the victims just as much. The fear and the damage caused by economic terrorism are no less than those of other forms of terror.

Dr Mahathir explains that Islam has nothing to do with terrorism. He pleads, on behalf of Muslims throughout the world, that those who have been quick to link Islam to terrorism should make an effort to understand Islam and the Muslims. He emphasises that Islam is a religion of peace, a tolerant religion which can coexist with any faith, quoting Malaysia as a case in point. But as with followers of other religions, there are Muslims who, for some reason or other, do not adhere to the teachings of Islam.

Without mincing his words, Dr Mahathir presents his views and opinions candidly. He analyses the issue by giving precise interpretations of the realities and points to the way towards how to handle the problem. He fears that as events unfold in Afghanistan, Iraq and Palestine, it is beginning to look more and more like a war against Islam.

This is a book by a great leader and thinker, recognised not only among emerging nations of the world but also by those who have a high regard for his courage in expressing his views where others have found it difficult to do so. It is more than just about terrorism. It is also about the disturbing prospects of the future and forewarning of its possible dangers and consequences.

Lt Gen (Rtd) Raja Dato' Abdul Rashid Raja Badiozaman
Former Chief of Defence Intelligence Staff

1

Understanding Islam and the Muslims

"... the Muslims of today seem to be isolating themselves and resorting to violence, but they are a minority. Despite the decline of the Muslim civilisation, the majority of Muslims throughout the world today still tolerate and show understanding of other religions and their adherents."

WE we are on the brink of a new millennium today. It is a good time to reflect seriously on what has happened and what might happen. The former, of course, is the easier of the two.

A speech delivered at the Seminar on "The Role of Islamic Civilisation in Fostering Interreligious Understanding", organised by the Institute of Islamic Understanding Malaysia (IKIM) in Kuala Lumpur, Malaysia, on May 25, 1999

The last time the world ushered in a new millennium, Islamic civilisation was perhaps at its peak. But as we approach the third millennium of the Christian era, Islamic civilisation seems to be at its lowest ebb. Muslims, although they have achieved political independence, are very much dominated by other people. Muslims are being massacred by the hundreds of thousands without their co-religionists being able to do anything to help. We should not be surprised therefore if it is difficult to believe that the Islamic religion and Islamic civilisation had played a role in interreligious understanding.

I say this because the present-day perception of Islam by both Muslims and non-Muslims is quite different and very often at variance with the teachings of Islam as practised by the early Muslims, particularly during the period when Muslims were revelling in their glorious civilisation.

Today, Muslims are seen to be aloof and isolated even when they live in communities which have large numbers of non-Muslims. They are seldom regarded as practising and contributing towards interreligious understanding.

The non-Muslims are at least partly to blame because they often propagate ideas about Islam and Muslims which are negative. Among ethnic Europeans the memories of the Crusade and the conquest of European land by Muslims many centuries ago are kept alive. Every fault of the Muslims is enlarged and linked with the religion even though it may have nothing to do with it. It is not acknowledged that Muslims are ordinary people divided by race and culture and are as subjected to ordinary human weaknesses as anybody else. Instead they are regarded as a monolithic group. This perception leads to frequent generalisations so that the crimes or misbehaviour of a few are attributed to the culture and practices of all Muslims.

Thus the stereotyping of Muslims as undisciplined backward people, unsociable, fanatical fundamentalists who are given to terrorism. That terrorism is not a monopoly of the Muslims is ignored entirely. Every terrorist act is attributed to Muslims until proven otherwise.

In terms of terror and systematic oppression, the ethnic Europeans have no match. Adolf Hitler's massacre of six million Jews during World War II ranks as the most heinous of crimes against humanity in the 20th century. And now we are witnessing the mass-killings of Albanians in Kosovo, which was preceded by the massacre of hundreds of thousands of Muslims in Bosnia-Herzegovina. Yet all these acts by ethnic Europeans are never described as European or Christian terrorism.

Even Buddhists have thrown up a number of terrorists as witnessed by the killings perpetrated by a shadowy Japanese Buddhist cult. Hindus have massacred Muslims off and on in India.

But acts of terrorism or even simple self-defence by Muslims in Palestine are invariably described as Muslim terrorism. The terrorists, if they are terrorists and in many instances they are not, are labelled Muslim terrorists. Terrorism by others, by ethnic Europeans, by intolerant Christians and Jews, and by Buddhists, are never linked to their religions. There are no Christian terrorists, or Jewish terrorists, or Buddhist terrorists, or Orthodox Christian terrorists, which the Serbs no doubt are.

That more Muslims have been terrorised by Christians and Jews has never been mentioned.

Terrorism is made out to be a Muslim monopoly and others are just terrorists unconnected with their ethnic group or culture or religion.

There can be no doubt that today the most oppressed people in the world are the Muslims. Their independence and their rights as members of the human race have been ignored and violated over and over again. Their countries have been subjected to sanctions, to bombings, and to all kinds of humiliation. Is it any wonder that Muslims seem to be perpetually resentful and antagonistic towards non-Muslims, to cut themselves off from the others and to reject the norms and the way of life that is common among the rest of the world? They seem to reject the religions of others and they do not seem to contribute to interreligious understanding.

But the Muslims are equally to be blamed for their ugly reputation, their poor image and their isolation. However, this has not always been so. The early Muslims were outgoing people who tolerated and associated closely with people of other religions. Islamic teachings did not and does not proscribe such tolerance and association. Islam, in fact, enjoins upon the Muslim to accept that there are people of different faiths who worship in different ways. They are not asked to force these people to accept Islam. Obviously, they must tolerate and understand these non-believers, not regard them as enemies.

What is it that is part of the teachings of Islam which the early Muslims practised? As has been pointed out the Quran specifically mentioned that there would be people of other faiths who worship in other ways. Indeed, the Quran went further to advise the Muslims that they should not be critical of or pass disparaging remarks about the practices of adherents of other religion for this may result in these people making similar remarks about Islam.

Forced conversion to Islam is not sanctioned by the Quran. Indeed, the Prophet was told not to be disheartened if non-Muslims did not convert, for if Allah so wishes, they would convert. If they didn't it was because Allah had not yet willed it. And indeed many of the early enemies of Islam accepted the faith.

The Quran also pointed out that Allah has populated the world with people of different races so they may know each other. And the Arabs were not superior to the others except when they prostrate before Allah and practise the teachings of Islam thoroughly and sincerely.

And so the early Muslims were not only tolerant of non-Muslims but in their search for knowledge as enjoined by Islam they were willing to study the sciences and the mathematical knowledge of the non-Muslims, in particular the Greeks. They translated Greek works into Arabic, studied them and developed them further. Soon their universities and their learned men were leading the world and the European Christians were seeking knowledge at their feet.

Islamic civilisation in Spain reached its peak of glory when Muslims were tolerant of others and were prepared to learn from them. In Muslim Spain, Christians, Jews and Muslims lived side by side. Many were the Jews and Christians who served in the courts of the Muslim rulers and in their governments.

Then came the decline, earlier in Spain than in Eastern Europe. Muslim religious intellectuals and jurists began to reinterpret the teachings of Islam. They postulate that the Muslims had departed from the teachings of Islam when they seek other than religious knowledge and associated with non-Muslims. The learning of the sciences and mathematics pioneered by the Christians was regarded as worldly and not desired by Islam. Instead, Muslims must lead a life dedicated entirely towards gaining merit for the life in the hereafter. Much stress was laid on Islamic jurisprudence, on punishment for those who had allegedly deviated from the religion. The Spanish and Jewish people who had converted to the Islamic faith were regarded with suspicion and toleration towards them began to diminish.

As the Muslims turned away from all learning which were not exclusively about religion, their skills deteriorated. They became weak and were unable to match the sophistication of European sciences, weaponry and military prowess. Eventually they lost their Spanish Empire. They were expelled from Spain unless they converted to Christianity.

The same fate later befell the Turkish Empire. At the height of their glory they were assailed by doubts about the quality of their Islam. While the Europeans modernised and were discovering new ways of defending themselves against the redoubtable Turkish forces, the Turks were concerned over trivialities such as whether tight trousers and peak caps were Islamic or not. Whereas the earlier Turkish forces were well equipped with the best weapons of their time, their knowledge and their industry did not keep up with the knowledge, industrial skills and manufacturing capabilities which were rapidly making the Europeans superior in all fields.

The Turkish religious leaders were only concerned about ensuring that their narrow interpretations of Islam were adhered to strictly by the state and the people. They were not concerned about the weakening of the Turkish state and its defence capability. Parts of the Empire peopled by non-Turks began to break away to establish independent states. The Europeans encouraged this and even aided the Arabs to fight for their independence from the Turks.

The Arabs expected to be independent but in the end they found that their European allies replaced the Turks as their masters. They all became colonies of the French and the British. In North Africa, Muslim lands were conquered and occupied by the Spanish and the French while in Central Asia the Russian communists imposed not only their rule but also their atheistic ideology on the Muslims.

By the time the Muslims realised that their days of glory were over, they had become an extremely backward and weak people. Initially they submitted meekly to foreign rule. They deluded themselves into believing that this worldly life is not for them and that heaven awaited them in the afterlife. That the Quran clearly states that they should seek *hassanah* (bounty) in this world was ignored by them. They expect to achieve merit for their afterlife purely through the performance of religious rituals. They ignored the injunction to look after their community's well-being and interest in this world, and they refused to acquire knowledge except those related to what they interpreted as the teachings of Islam.

And so from being the most knowledgeable and advanced people the Muslims regressed in every field. Hegemonised and oppressed by the non-Muslims they developed extreme resentment and hatred of their detractors. They blamed their enemies entirely for their misfortunes. They hardly ever examined and questioned their own role in their downfall and subsequent oppression.

Actually their downfall was at least partly due to their narrow interpretation of their own religion after the initial flowering of their civilisation. Discarding the so-called worldly knowledge and quibbling about what constituted the true teachings of Islam, they neglected some of the most important injunctions of Islam. They neglected even the injunction to prepare for their defence by taking the word of the Quran too literally.

True, the Quran enjoined upon the Muslim to strike fear among their enemies by readying their war steeds and their swords. If the Quran had mentioned steel tanks, rockets, aircraft, bombs and guns, the teachings of Islam would not have been credible, much less accepted by the ignorant Arab at the time of the Prophet. To ready horses and swords was more understandable in the days of the Prophet. But the real message of the Quran is to deter the enemy with a credible defence force. Had this message been understood then, the Muslims would not have forsaken the study of the sciences and other allegedly worldly learnings necessary for the invention and production of the ever-changing weapons for defence.

The result is the defeat of the once mighty Muslim armies and the fall of all Muslim lands to the European. Having fallen they still failed to diagnose the cause of their downfall. They went on with their endless debate on Islam, Islamic jurisprudence and Islamic practices. This debate only lead to their fragmentation as new sects, cults and teachings threw up frequently antagonistic groups. Even the achievement of national independence did not result in the realisation of the need to acquire the skills and knowledge to defend the country and the religion and to catch up with the progress of the developed countries. Instead everywhere there was a tussle between the religiously educated and those educated in other disciplines for control of the state apparatus. There can be no doubt that the desire for power was not motivated by religion as much as personal greed and ambition.

As most Muslims are religiously inclined, each side tried to outdo the other by professing to be guided by the teachings of Islam. Each tried to be more Islamic than the others. That what they were doing was against the true teachings of Islam did not deter those who saw in their profession of faith a means of getting popular support and power.

The rallying cry of the orthodox religiously trained group is 'secularism'. Anything at all that is not directly concerned with worship, rituals and the gaining of merit for oneself is classified as secular and therefore irreligious or anti-religion.

It is unfortunate that Mustafa Kemal Attartuk, the Turkish patriot, had wrongly blamed Islam and not the narrow interpretation of Islam as the cause of the collapse of the Turkish Empire. Believing that the solution to Turkey's problems lie in the rejection of Islam, Mustafa Kemal made secularism the Turkish state creed. Islam was proscribed in his belief that to be secular the Islamic religion must in no way influence the affairs of state. Thus he expected the country he had saved from Greek occupation would be like the European countries where there was a separation between the Church and the State. He attributed the progress and success of the Europeans to this separation and the secularisation of the governments.

Mustafa Kemal's secularisation of Turkey angered the Muslims in Turkey and the Muslim world in general. They attributed it to associating and accepting European (Christian) values. They accordingly developed a fear of whatever was regarded by them as secular. In their anger and fear they did not pause to think about what was meant by secularism. They certainly did not examine it in the context of Islam.

Separation of Church and State, separation between the secular and the religious may be possible in Christianity. But it is impossible in Islam. Islam is a way of life and a way of life cannot be confined to pure worship and rituals only. It cannot be about the hereafter entirely. A way of life must involve everything that we do in our daily life.

Thus the study of science and technology is related to the provision of a good life for Muslims and certainly is concerned with the safety and defence of the Muslim *ummah*. Doing business and acquiring wealth is also for the well-being of the *ummah* in this world for how else can the alms, and the *zakat* be expected to help the needy. Even improving the means of travel is related to the performance of the Haj. Today millions of Muslims are able to perform the Haj because of the new modes of transportation developed by non-Muslims. The Muslims cannot claim they made this contribution to the performance of the Haj.

The development and the prosperity of the Muslim country, good government, a good and just legal system, rules and regulation and laws, indeed everything that has to do in this world, is a part of the way of life. The only thing that is required is that they do not go against the injunctions of Islam, that they do not lead to such arrogance that it denies that God exists. The communists, for example, are so taken up by human skills and power that they reject God and religion.

The way of life of the Muslim does not include being ignorant, being without modern knowledge, being without skills, being poor and being forced to buy from others, including from those whom they regard as being secular, for sustenance and for defence. Surely the present inability of Muslims to protect other Muslims who are being butchered and expelled from their countries is not in keeping with the Muslim way of life. And yet the inability of the Muslim to protect other Muslims in distress is entirely due to their backwardness and their general poverty.

There is nothing secular about learning the sciences, the skills and the technologies that can undoubtedly contribute towards the well-being and the safety of the Muslims. Merit for the hereafter does not come from the performance of various rituals and worship and the study of religious matters alone. The whole community of Muslims will be committing a sin if none of them is able to perform *fardu kifayah* (i.e., to provide for the needs of the Muslims' well-being in this world).

The lack of understanding of secularism within the Muslim context and the fear of a repeat of the Turkish 'secularisation' has resulted in Muslims becoming ignorant and backward and incapable of defending themselves. The blame must be put squarely on the Muslims for their inability to perform an essential part of the teachings of Islam.

But the fear of secularisation has lead Muslims into trying to insulate themselves from outside influences. To do this they try to physically isolate themselves from non-Muslims. This they do by propagating the fear that contact with non-Muslims will lead to contamination of their religion and what they regard as their Islamic way of life. As a result they do not contribute towards interreligious understanding as was done by the early Muslims.

In Malaysia today, there is a disturbing trend among religious teachers to influence children into avoiding contact with non-Muslims. Because Muslims should only eat what is *halal*, teachers try to create fear among children that they may be eating food that is not *halal*. They create such doubts in the minds of children that they do not trust even the food prepared in their own homes and in restaurants where their parents take them to.

Such a condition leads to a fear that association with non-Muslims would cause them to be contaminated with what is *haram* to Islam. In a country where there is a substantial number of non-Muslims, Muslim children are being taught to keep away from non-Muslims, to be unsociable. They cannot therefore contribute towards interreligious understanding.

This attempt to isolate Muslims from non-Muslims is not limited to kindergartens. Today, in schools and universities, Muslim students are urged to keep to themselves, to avoid activities which cannot be confined to Muslim students only. As a result it is rare for Muslim students to have non-Muslim friends, something that can contribute to interreligious understanding.

The old generation was gregarious. They mixed well with non-Muslims and they were able to interact with them without in any way becoming any less Muslim. But we see the new generation already quite unable to adjust to a multiracial and multireligious country.

This insulation and isolation will not help foster interreligious understanding. Indeed, in multiracial, multireligious Malaysia, these Muslims are not going to be able to adjust and live harmoniously and to benefit from the numerous and varied opportunities such an environment offers for the prosperity and advancement of Muslims. And what is happening in Malaysia, in terms of isolating and insulating Muslims ostensibly in order to preserve the purity of their religion, is happening all over the Muslim world. If today Muslims are misunderstood and are unable to create understanding of themselves and their religion, it is because they chose to create this misunderstanding by keeping themselves apart and so are unable to show the true teachings of Islam.

But isolating and insulating themselves is not all that the Muslims do to cause the non-Muslims to have a biased and unfriendly view of them. The oppression of Muslims in many parts of the world, in Palestine, Eastern Europe and elsewhere, has caused deep bitterness and anger among them. Unable to fight back because their countries are weak, many have resorted to violence, to acts which are described as terroristic, in order to vent their anger and frustration.

They very quickly learnt the methods of terrorism invented in the West. They hijack airplanes, they bomb buildings, they kill people, innocent and otherwise, and they indulge in other violent activities in order to further their cause.

Unfortunately, their cause is not served but they do bring about greater condemnation and misunderstanding of their religion and the Muslim people.

Today, as has been pointed out earlier, Islam and Muslims have been made almost synonymous with terrorism. The whole world has this perception of Islam and Muslims. It is as if Islam itself advocates irresponsible terroristic acts.

Between their use of their religion to isolate themselves and their violent reaction to oppression, Muslims have contributed much to the lack of understanding between them and the followers of other religions. But does Islam teach Muslims to isolate themselves, to create misunderstanding between them and the others?

Actually, Islam does not teach this or advocate the isolation and the insulation of the religion. From the very beginning the Prophet and the Muslims were made to understand that Allah created the peoples of this world of different races and kinds so that they may know each other. These people and even the Arabs may not all accept Islam. The Quran clearly states that there will be those who will worship in their own way and their religion would be theirs. Their refusal to accept Islam must be accepted. The Prophet must accept this because his duty was to spread the message. If Allah so wishes then everyone would embrace Islam. If they don't it is Allah's wish and the Prophet need not despair.

In other words, Muslims must accept that there will be people of many races and creeds who profess different religions and that they are so created that they may know each other, i.e., that there should be understanding between peoples of different religions.

And so the first Muslim community in Madinah (Medina) was able to live among the Hebrews and the Christians. No attempt was made to force the others to become Muslims. If later on the Jews were expelled from Madinah it was because they abetted and sided with the enemies who attacked Madinah and the Muslims. It was not because of religious differences.

The early Muslims conquered many lands where the people were of other religions and these people retained their faiths to this day. In Muslim Spain, Jews and Christians were able to practise their religions and way of life, and even participate in the administration of the country. It is significant that following the reconquest of Spain by Ferdinand and Isabella, non-Catholics disappeared. Jews and Muslims either accepted Catholicism or migrated to Muslim North Africa.

In Eastern Europe, the Christians were happy to accept Turkish Muslim rule because of the very heavy taxes imposed by their former Christian rulers. These Christians remained as Christians although a few chose to embrace Islam.

It is a testimony to Muslim tolerance and understanding that in practically all countries ruled by Muslims there was and there still is a significant non-Muslim minority. By contrast the European countries had in the past only an insignificant number of Jews and almost no Muslim or people of other religions. Whereas the Jews thrived and even prospered in Muslim countries, they were subjected to periodical pogroms in Europe. This culminated in the Holocaust when some six million Jews were massacred.

The early Muslims adhered closely to the teachings of Islam which recognise the rights of the *Dhimmi*, non-Muslims who had no quarrel with Muslims. Right through the period of Islamic glory, non-Muslims were not only tolerated but played important roles in Muslim countries.

This tolerance and cooperation with non-Muslims began with the Madinah Charter enacted by the Prophet which encouraged solidarity among Muslims, Jews and Christians of the City of Madinah. Succeeding Caliphs all showed tolerance and understanding of non-Muslims and their religions. After the surrender of Jerusalem, the Caliph Omar in the treaty of surrender assured Sophronius, the Patriarch of the City, that "The Caliph Omar guarantees (the Christian) the safety of their persons, their goods, their churches and crosses, whether in good state or otherwise and in general their religion. Their church will not be turned into dwellings or destroyed ..., etc." And the Caliph honoured his treaty undertakings. Even on his deathbed Omar reminded Muslims to show kindness to their non-Muslim neighbours.

The same terms and conditions were granted by Muslim leaders to the inhabitants of Damascus, al-Hijrah and others. Count Leon Ostrorog, a Western scholar, wrote, "The Muslim thinkers of the Ninth Century have expanded a doctrine of toleration of non-Muslims."

The culture of tolerance of other religions and faiths developed by the Islamic civilisation was totally in keeping with the teachings of Islam. This tolerance was not passive. In medicine, Jewish and Christian doctors worked closely with Muslim doctors and produced medical research works together. Even comparative religion was studied together by the scholars of the three monotheistic religions.

In administration, the Muslim rulers of the Umayad, Amirid and Taifa periods employed Jews in diplomacy, finance and public administration. Hasday ibn Shaprut was a Jewish physician in the Caliph's court and he openly looked after the interest of Jews in Muslim Spain.

This practice of employing Jews in positions of importance was found also in the Fatimid, Ayyubid and even the Mamluk periods.

Further East, the Muslims came into contact with polytheistic religions. Although there was practically no reference to these religions and their adherents in the Quran, the Muslims found little difficulty in according them the same treatment that they gave the monotheists. Thus Hindus and Buddhists were able to thrive in lands conquered and ruled by Muslims. That this is so is seen from the existence of Buddhists and Hindus in lands still ruled or formerly ruled by Muslims.

When the Sultan of Malacca embraced Islam he did cause to be destroyed all the Hindu temples where his people used to worship. But there is no evidence that he forced the foreign Hindus and Buddhists in his country to convert to Islam or to destroy their places of worship. And so to this day these people, although they had adopted the Malay language and culture, retained their religious beliefs.

This tolerance and understanding of other religions, as has been pointed out, is a part of the teaching of Islam. Throughout history this teaching was accepted and practised. Of course, like other teachings, there were, in practice, frequent deviations and distortions. Those with their own agenda may twist the interpretations in order to serve their purpose. And so throughout history and also presently there would be incidents of interreligious misunderstanding between Muslims and others. But these merely serve to prove the rule.

Islamic civilisation has indeed contributed much towards interreligious understanding. This is borne by the fact that whereas in Muslim countries there are almost always thriving and prosperous non-Muslim communities, in most non-Muslim countries only one religion is found and practised. It is only lately that mosques and temples are found in Europe and America, for example. It is also significant that there are hardly any Europeans who are Muslim, Buddhist or Hindu.

This is not an attempt to make comparisons or to say that non-Muslims and the civilisations that they built contribute less towards interreligious understanding. It is merely to emphasise that Islam and Muslims believe more in religious tolerance and understanding than they are made out to be.

It has been pointed out that the Muslims of today seem to be isolating themselves and resorting to violence, but they are a minority. Despite the decline of the Muslim civilisation, the majority of Muslims throughout the world today still tolerate and show understanding of other religions and their adherents. Thus in Bosnia, despite the massacre of Muslims by the Serbs, the Muslims never wavered from their objective of building a multireligious nation in which the Serbs have an active share in the government. The same is true of Lebanon. With few exceptions, in Muslim-majority countries throughout the world, non-Muslims are free to practise their own religions. And in Malaysia the Muslim Malays who make up the majority have deliberately opted to form multiracial and multireligious governments which work assiduously for interreligious tolerance and understanding.

Islam and the Islamic civilisation have indeed contributed much towards interreligious understanding. This is the direct result of the teachings of Islam. It is perhaps difficult to acknowledge this but it is nevertheless true. If there are Muslims who seem not to be contributing towards interreligious understanding today it is not because of the Islamic civilisation or the Islamic religion. It is because circumstances have given rise to many misinterpretation and deviations from the true teachings of Islam and because Islamic civilisation has declined somewhat.

2

The need to identify terrorists and remove the causes of terrorism

"Terrorists are not people who advertise their intention to commit acts of terror. They are not usually soldiers in uniform, although some can be. Usually they are unrecognisable until they commit their terrible acts."

TERRORISTS have been with us throughout history. Over the last half a century, terrorists have become more sophisticated and are much more focused. We may not agree with them, we may consider them misguided but it would be a mistake to think that they terrorise for the sake of terrorism, or

---

A speech delivered at the Conference on Terrorism in Kuala Lumpur, Malaysia, on November 16, 2001

because they enjoy terrorising their victims. Their evil deeds have a purpose, to them at least. They would not willingly kill themselves in the most horrible fashion on September 11 if it is not because they believe there is a purpose for their suicide.

And so, whether we like it or not, we have to learn to understand their psyche if we want to deal with them, if we want to counter them, if we want to eliminate them, if we want to stop terrorism.

But, first, we must determine who a terrorist is. This is important because people who some people describe as terrorists are regarded as noble freedom fighters by some others. More confusing still, some are condemned as terrorists one day, only to be considered respectable people another day. If we want the whole world to join in the fight against terrorists then we must ensure that a terrorist is a terrorist to all and everyone at all times.

Examples of the ambivalence in the definition of terrorists are many. The Jewish Haganah, Irgun Zeva'i Le'umi and Stern Gang were at one time regarded as terrorists and were hunted by the British. But later they became respected leaders of Israel. Jomo Kenyatta and Robert Mugabe were described as terrorists and were condemned by the British only to become in the end the acknowledged leaders of independent states.

The Irish Republican Army (IRA) is a terrorist organisation in the eyes of the British but are regarded as freedom fighters worthy of financial support by the Americans.

With such differences in the views of different people at different times, it is difficult to get the whole world to join in the fight against terrorism. And if the whole world is not in the fight and the hunt, if some people and some countries provide shelter and protection for the terrorists because in their eyes these are not terrorists, it would be impossible to eliminate or liquidate the terrorists and to put an end to terrorism.

The operative word here is terror. Terrorists use terror as their weapon. The hijacking and crashing of the aircrafts create terror in the minds of people, especially the direct and indirect victims. Such is the fear created that people are now afraid to fly. The Abu Sayyaf kidnappers inspire fear by beheading their hostages. Exploding bombs in public places and killing innocent people inspire fear and terror, and a feeling of being unsafe anywhere at any time. Unexpected death stares everyone in the face without one knowing it and being able to take evasive measures.

Poisoning through chemicals or gas frighten people. Killing children and non-combatants, taking hostages, etc. all bring about fear and terror among people.

If we have to determine who a terrorist is and who is not then we have to base it on the act—not on the person, the group, the race or the religion.

Once we agree on what constitutes an act of terror, then it would be easy to identify a terrorist. Even if his cause is noble, even if he is fighting against oppression, against terrorists themselves, using acts of terror would not be justified. He becomes a terrorist. And as a terrorist he should be outlawed by the world, should be hunted, captured, tried and appropriately punished.

At the moment, Osama bin Laden and his followers are considered to be terrorists. Admittedly, at the moment they are the prime suspects and they should be hunted. But despite protests that the war against terrorists is not a war against Islam, what cannot be denied is that only Muslim terrorists are being targeted.

In Palestine, civilians, including children, are being shot and killed every day by Israelis. And in retaliation the Palestinians kill Israelis with human bombs at times. Every day Palestinians face the possibility of being killed. Can it be said that they do not live in terror of being the next victim? Yes, the Israelis too, but they have superior firepower and obviously they instil more terror in the hearts of Palestinians than the other way round.

Then there are the Bosnians, the Chechens, the Iraqis, the people of Kosovo—all living or had lived in fear of being killed. Are we to dismiss their terror as of no consequence? Are we just going to hunt for the collaborators of the September 11 attacks and ignore the other acts of terror?

The Afghans must be living in a state of terror, waiting for the bombs to rain on them, to maim and kill them, their children and their friends. Can we say that because other innocent people had been killed therefore it is right to retaliate by killing other innocent people? Terrorists are unprincipled, despicable people. Should civilised people do unprincipled, despicable things because the terrorists did?

And now there is talk of extending the war to other countries. Iraq should receive the same treatment as Afghanistan even if there is no evidence that they harboured the prime suspect and his followers. There is some evidence, as vague as the evidence against Osama bin Laden, that anthrax were being spread not by Muslim Arabs but by violently rightist Christians. We must remember that Timothy McVeigh who blew up the government building in Oklahoma belonged to such a group. Yet while there is talk about attacking Iraq there is no violent rage against the spreaders of anthrax or McVeigh's supporters. We hate to say it but it is beginning to look more and more like a war against Muslims.

This impression can only be got rid of if actions are taken also against those people who terrorise the Muslims, e.g. against the Israelis in Palestine. Perhaps the world is not prepared to punish the Israelis. But at least the world can take action to protect the Palestinians, to separate them from the Israelis.

Terrorists are not people who advertise their intention to commit acts of terror. They are not usually soldiers in uniform, although some can be. Usually they are unrecognisable until they commit their terrible acts. Usually they are like ordinary people. They need not stay in a particular country. They can be everywhere and anywhere. Indeed they can live as very ordinary people in the country they consider to be their enemy, against whom they intend to commit acts of terror.

Today we can safely assume that the associates of those involved in the September 11 attacks are not just in Afghanistan. Today we can assume that they are in the U.S. in Europe or in any of the Muslim or non-Muslim countries. Because we do not know who they are or where they are it is difficult to wage a conventional war against them. Afghanistan may be harbouring them, but it is not necessary that they will be under the control of the Afghans. Even if the Afghans want to, they may not be able to hand over the terrorists to the people who are after them.

Attacking Afghanistan is not going to result in the killing or capture of the terrorists. Wiping out the Afghans, reducing their country to dust will not wipe out the terrorists. Some may be killed but many others living outside Afghanistan or who have slipped out of

Afghanistan would escape unscathed. Safe and alive, they can still carry out acts of terror. They are not likely to be deterred by the killings of the Afghans or the destruction of the country.

On the other hand, the killing of the Afghans and the destruction of that country is likely to anger a lot of Muslims. Their governments may not, though it is very likely that they too could be angered by the wanton acts against a brother Muslim country. But certainly the vast majority of the Muslims in whichever country are going to get very angry. And of the many millions of angry Muslims there would be quite a few who would join the ranks of the terrorists and be willing to die to avenge what is to them a gross injustice and cruelty. And so the bombings and rocketing of Afghanistan, far from progressing the war to eliminate terrorists would actually result in the spawning of more terrorists. The world is going to be saddled with the terrorist problem forever. And we don't know what new villainy they would think of.

Malaysia is familiar with terrorism and the war against terrorists. Rebel-trained guerrillas believe that guerrillas can never be defeated. By their books the terrorists in Malaysia could not be defeated. But we defeated them. After fighting for 42 years, between 1948 and 1990, the terrorists in Malaysia decided to lay down arms.

Why did they do so? They laid down arms because the government of Malaysia did not just fight them with arms. We did not just chase them into the jungles and out of Malaysia. We did not just force them to resort to the plastic mines and ambushes. We carried out a campaign to win the hearts and minds of the people so as to ensure that the terrorists lost their civilian support.

We studied the causes of the disaffection of these terrorists and their supporters and we took remedial action. Our decision to accord citizenship rights to over a million non-Malays was not regarded as a victory for the struggle of the terrorists but rather as a means to win the loyalty of disaffected people and to get them to join in the war against the terrorists. This act and others helped to mobilise the people of Malaysia to defeat the terrorists.

Similarly, in the fight against terrorists and terrorism, the causes of the anger and frustration of the terrorists must be studied and action taken to remove these causes. I believe that the principal cause is the Palestinian issue. Israelis believe they have a historical claim to the land of Palestine but prior to the deliberate settlement of Jews in Palestine there were only six thousand Jews against over 300,000 Arabs. The settlement of Jews after World War II not only reduced the Arab majority, but forced more than a million Arabs to be displaced and to live in miserable tent cities for over 50 years. Their futile attempts to regain Arab land only resulted in the Palestinians losing their own State.

After tens of thousands of them had died, they do not even have a right to their own independent State. Their land has been seized by the Israelis who built settlements on these lands. Arab houses were bulldozed and the occupants forced to evacuate. All the while Arabs were killed with impunity and reported in the world press as retaliation for Arab attacks against the Jews. Actually the Arab attacks were retaliation for Jewish attacks on the Palestinians. What is an undeniable fact is that more Palestinians are killed than Jews. Still the Palestinians were described as terrorists and their peace overtures were rejected.

Although initially the Arabs refused to recognise an Israeli State, their subsequent recognition did not result in any relenting on the part of the Israelis. The Israelis refused to recognise the State of Palestine. In frustration the Palestinian restarted the *intifada* (or *intifadeh*). Again stones were thrown at Israeli forces by Palestinian children. The Israelis replied with live bullets, machine-gunfire and rocket attacks. Children were killed along with those who were defending the Palestinian state.

There is no sign of the fighting coming to an end. International pressure to cease fighting is not practical. Even if Yasser Arafat agreed to a ceasefire, he cannot possibly stop his people, individuals, bitter at having lost their children or members of their family or their friends, from continuing to attack and kill the Israelis. Each attack by Arabs invariably resulted in more Arabs than Israelis being killed. And the Israelis would attack the Arabs with deadly accuracy. And the Arabs would retaliate ineffectively.

We can say that it is because of Arab attacks that the Israelis have to retaliate. But such retaliation will not solve the Arab-Israeli conflict. Only forcible separation of the two people by a strong United Nations (U.N.) peacekeeping force can do this. The Palestinians are willing to have the U.N. peacekeeping force but the Israelis and their supporters object. And the world pander to the wishes of the Israelis. And so the killings and terror continue.

In the Muslim world there is a great deal of anger which the West cannot understand. But the Muslim world, weak and unable to be of any help to the Palestinians see in the unwillingness of the West to stop the Israelis as a sign that the West is anti-Palestine, anti-Arab and anti-Muslim.

Most Muslims will only feel anger, will talk but will do nothing. But among the billion Muslims there must be those whose anger cannot be contained. These are the people who will resort to terror tactics.

It is reasonable to believe that if there is no Palestinian issue, if the Palestinian are not being oppressed and children being killed, the anger of the Arabs and Muslims would not be there or would be much less. Certainly there would not be those who would be willing to kill themselves in that horrible fashion on September 11.

The belief that these terrorists act in that manner because of poverty or because of jealousy for the good life and the freedom of other people does not reflect a deep knowledge of the terrorist mind. Those who hijacked and crashed the aircrafts are not fanatical illiterates who only see heaven in the afterlife. These people come from the richer Muslim countries, countries where generous governments give allowances and subsidise the life of the people. These are people who are married and have wives and children. They must know that the course they are taking would separate them permanently from their families, friends and a good life. And yet, apparently, they are prepared to die in a horrible fashion as they steered their aircrafts towards the World Trade Center.

We must not glorify these terrorists. But we need to understand their minds and their mentality. We need to do this if we want to understand the reason why they did this. If we don't then we will not be able to remove the causes and reduce the incidence of terrorism.

Revenge is sweet. But if we are going to liquidate the culprits almost completely as is likely to happen if we simply bomb and rocket Afghanistan then we won't even achieve the revenge that we are after. The terrorists will probably feel sorry that they had brought death and destruction to their host but they are more likely to feel angrier and to be more determined to continue with their acts of terror. There is no revenge.

But in fighting terrorism one must not think of revenge. One must think of ways to make the world free of terrorists. And that is going to require careful strategy.

If the whole world, including the Muslim world, is to be asked to participate in the elimination of terrorists and terrorism, then all terrorists, irrespective of their race or religion or the particular acts of terrorism that they were involved in, must be the target for elimination. And these must include state terrorists as well, including the Israeli government of Ariel Sharon, the man responsible for the massacre of thousands of Palestinians in Sabra and Shatila and is still the man behind the systematic killing of Palestinians today. No terrorists should be spared; it does not matter whether their cause is right or not.

The world must be serious about the fight against terrorists. It will never be completely wiped out but it certainly can be reduced and rendered less frightening for the world. Because of the attacks on September 11, the whole world's economy has been thrown into recession. The cost of turning around the world's economy will be very, very high but at every turn the possibility of terror attacks has to be gauged and costly counter measures provided for. It is far better to spend that money to reduce or eliminate terrorism than to try and live in fear of terror attacks at a very high cost.

We used to talk of the balance of terror. This refers to the nuclear arms held by the East-West blocs in the Cold War. Today the terror comes not from great nuclear powers but from individuals and groups whose capacity to do damage is out of all proportion to their financial capacity or their technological capacity. But they hold the balance of terror. Perhaps the great powers with their command of sophisticated technology and unlimited finance may be able to tilt the balance of terror in their favour again. But we cannot bank on it, not in the near future anyway.

To eliminate the terrorists we must know who they are. Race, religion and country cannot be used to identify the terrorists. We can only identify terrorists by their acts. Unfortunately, by the time they commit their crime it is too late. If the whole world cooperates we can determine who their compatriots, collaborators or supporters are. The world must support action taken specifically against these criminals.

But identifying and hunting the terrorists will be very difficult and will take a long time. The better immediate solution is to remove the causes of terrorism. We may not want to remove these causes because we do not like to give the impression that the terrorists have succeeded. But such an attitude will not help. The terrorists must be hunted and brought to justice but the causes of their committing the acts of terror must be removed.

Once the causes have been removed, support for the terrorists will be much reduced if not cease altogether. And as in the case of Malaysia, once the terrorists lost their support base, sooner or later they must give up their activity. Even terrorists would not want to sacrifice their lives for nothing, and removing the cause will mean their sacrifices would be for nothing.

Everyone is exposed to terror attacks whether they are in any way involved or not. It is therefore in everyone's interest to seek a solution to this problem.

You may not find the ultimate solution but you are certain to throw up ideas on how to deal with this terrible problem of the 21st century, ideas which we can study and develop and in due course help us put an end to this scourge.

3

Islam, terrorism and Malaysia's response

"Malaysia can claim to know how to deal with terrorists, be they Muslims or non-Muslims. We have been successful so far and we believe we can successfully handle future problems."

IN the first place I must insist that terrorism is not an Islamic monopoly. In Malaysia, for 42 long years we fought communist guerrillas which employed terror tactics in Malaysia to force the acceptance of the ideology. We defeated it.

A speech delivered at the Asia Society Dinner in New York, United States, on February 4, 2002

We defeated it not just through military action but more by winning the hearts and minds of the people who supported them. Since the terrorists were ethnic Chinese we identified the causes of their disaffection and remedied them. The result was a swing in favour of the government and we eventually put an end to Malaysian terrorism.

One can say the same of terrorists anywhere, including those who are Muslim by religion. Islam does not promote terrorism. Islam is a religion of peace. But when Muslims feel they are being oppressed, when they are not getting a fair deal, then they react very much like the ethnic Chinese in Malaysia reacted.

While we must condemn their acts of terror we must also strive to understand the reasons for their anger and their reactions, irrational though they may be. We must understand why if we are going to tackle the problem.

The terrorists of today are not wild-eyed, illiterate fanatics who merely obey the orders of their evil leaders. They are educated, well-off, normal people with wives and families to love and look after. We wouldn't know they are terrorists until they have committed their horrible crimes. Their known leaders and their group may be eliminated but until the causes are removed there is no guarantee new groups will not form to commit further acts of terror.

And so while we fight against the known or suspected terrorists we must eliminate the causes.

Why is it that of late acts of terror seem to be more frequently committed by the followers of Islam, the Muslims. In the first place, only Muslim terrorists are linked to their religion. No one ever mentioned the religions of the terrorists of Northern Ireland, of Sri

Lanka, of Japan, of Germany and of many other countries or people. But if they are Muslims they are always called Muslim terrorists. When Muslims in Bosnia-Herzegovina were being slaughtered by the Serbs there was no mention of Christian Orthodox terrorists. These Christian Orthodox terrorists killed far more people than were killed on September 11, 2001. The world did not mobilise to fight Christian Orthodox terrorists even when they terrorise the Kosovars.

Secondly, many Muslims are involved in acts of terror simply because presently Muslims and the Islamic countries are being oppressed most. In Bosnia-Herzegovina, Palestine, Iraq, Somalia, Sudan, Libya, Iran, India and Chechnya, it is the Muslims who are the injured parties. In fact, their terrorism is their reaction to what is to them acts of terror against them. But we are given the impression that Muslims are natural terrorists, that Islam advocates irrational acts of terror. But Islam is against the killing of innocent people, which, in the final analysis, is what terrorism is about.

If Muslims commit acts of terror, it is because their countries are weak and incapable of fighting back, of waging formal wars on their enemies. And so terrorism by Muslims is more common than by others. If there are Muslim countries as powerful as their enemies they would be bombing and rocketing regardless of what is now referred to as collateral damage.

Clearly Islam the religion is not the cause of terrorism. Islam, as I said, is a religion of peace. However, through the centuries, deviations from the true teachings of Islam have taken place. And so Muslims kill despite the injunction of their religion against killing, especially of innocent people.

If you look at Christianity you must admit that being thrown to the lions by the Romans did not prevent Christians when they achieved power from being totally intolerant of those who did not accept Christianity. During the Spanish Inquisition (1478-1834) suspected apostates were burnt at the stake after mock trials. In fact, many who are in America today are descended from Christians who had fled from terror perpetrated by other Christians. And the Jews in America are the descendants of the Jews who fled the regular pogroms in European countries especially Russia and of course the persecution by the Germans under Hitler.

Islam had, in fact, been more tolerant. The Jews chose to migrate to North Africa together with the defeated Muslims after Ferdinand and Isabella completed the reconquest of Spain. To stay back meant forced conversion to Christianity or the pain of death. Even after conversion they remained suspects and were persecuted.

The Muslims were well disposed towards Christians in particular. When the early Muslims were persecuted by the heathen Arabs, they seek refuge in Abyssinia (now Ethiopia), a Christian country with a Christian king. They were well treated there because the Christians realised they worshiped the same God and recognised not only the prophets of the Christians but those of the Jews as well. The Muslims venerate Musa (or Moses), and Isa (or Jesus) as their prophets along with Adam, Abraham, Jacob and others.

They differ from the Hebrews and the Christians because they believe that at the time of the Prophet Muhammad, the Jews and the Christians had deviated from the true teachings. But then you must remember that Martin Luther and others too accused the

Christians of their times of deviation from the true teachings and founded their own creed or sect in protest. So the Muslims' attitude towards Christianity is not much different from that of the various Protestant sects. In the past, Catholics and Protestants were violently intolerant of each other.

Islam is capable of coexisting with Judaism and Christianity if they are not oppressed. Indeed, Islam is capable of coexisting with other religions too, including those without any religion.

In Malaysia we have a truly incompatible mix of Hindus, Buddhists and Taoists, and Muslims, with a small Christian minority thrown in. Strictly speaking, we cannot even sit at the same table to eat. Muslims violently object to pork which the Chinese love but Muslims love beef which the Hindus do not eat. But we can and we do sit at the same table to eat because we are sensitive towards each other's sensitivities.

In Malaysia, Muslims, Hindus, Buddhists and Christians live together, work together and play together. In 1969 there were so-called race riots but the basic cause was economic rather than racial or religious. Once we reduce the economic disparities we were able to live in harmony with each other. Having a Muslim majority has not been a problem in Malaysia. Such is the harmony achieved by removing economic disparities that the recession due to the financial crisis failed to explode into religious or race riots as happened in other countries.

Now, there is an attempt by a small group of Muslim Malays to mount a violent struggle to take over the government of the country. They are almost all young members of the opposition Pan Malaysia Islamic Party (PMIP). These young people do not believe that democratic elections would ever bring their party to power, so they can install their version of an Islamic country.

The majority of them are religious students who went to Pakistan ostensibly to study Islam. Instead they were taught that the Malaysian government is not Islamic and it is their duty to overthrow it by violence. Trained by the Taliban and Osama bin Laden's people they returned to Malaysia to carry out their revolution.

In Malaysia, they killed a Christian state assemblyman, tried to steal arms from a police station, robbed banks and detonated ineffectively a few bombs in odd places. But eventually they were tracked down and arrested.

We have dealt with the would-be Muslim terrorists with circumspection. The majority of the people of Malaysia, Muslims and non-Muslims, support the government's action. We do not need foreign help or intervention. We are capable of dealing with any eventuality. The opposition Islamic party knows this and they are unlikely to back violence. However, if they break any of our laws, the fact that they are in the opposition will not prevent the government from enforcing the laws on them.

Malaysia can claim to know how to deal with terrorists, be they Muslims or non-Muslims. We have been successful so far and we believe we can successfully handle future problems. In fact, we think that we can be of help in dealing with modern terrorism elsewhere. I am sure our approach is more likely to be successful than the brute force that is being applied now. We know the people we call terrorists may be regarded as freedom fighters by others. Even today terrorists are regarded by their own people as noble freedom fighters. And of course terrorists like Jomo

Kenyatta, Mugabe, Nujoma and Mandela are now acknowledged as legitimate leaders of their countries.

However, whether people are fighting a noble cause or not there are certain acts which they may not perpetrate. Detonating bombs in public places and killing innocent people cannot be condoned. Holding civilians to ransom or as hostages cannot be accepted. Poisoning food, medicine or water supply cannot be accepted. These are all acts of terror and anyone committing these must be regarded as terrorists by everyone irrespective of the causes they are fighting for, irrespective of their religion, race or creed. And once they are defined as terrorists it is the duty of everyone, every country to hunt them down and bring them to justice.

Malaysia's response to the latest manifestation of terrorism is not only to act against our own potential terrorists but to seek to define terrorism and terrorists so that there is no ambiguity and everyone will be able to fight against them. We should not seek to avenge particular killings of innocent people. We should seek to fight all terrorists everywhere and we should fight them not just by direct action but more by winning the hearts and minds of the people so as to reduce support for acts of terrorism and to reduce the attraction of acts of terror for those who see no means of redress for their own sufferings.

4

Terrorism is as globalised as trade and investment

"The terrorism that assails the world today has a direct connection with the fate of the Palestinians. Terror has become as globalised as trade and investment. The law and policymakers of the world cannot limit their interest to their countries alone. They have to be interested in the whole world. That is why it is useful for them to come together and discuss their national problems as international issues, as problems which affect the whole world."

THE wars to end wars have been fought twice in the 20th century and have been won by the forces claiming to love peace. But we have never really been free from wars. Perhaps not on the scale of World War I and World War II but for many countries and people the wars they have to experience, the wars

---

A speech delivered at the Asia Society Dinner in New York, United States, on February 4, 2002

of liberation and the wars to protect their freedom are no less fearsome and damaging. Thousands have died in Eastern Europe, the Middle East, in Central and South America, in East Asia and South Asia, and in Africa. For many, peace is still an elusive goal.

The League of Nations had failed and the United Nations has not performed much better. The strong will dominate and the weak must submit. It is still a world of might is right.

The former colonies of the Europeans may have gained independence in the legal sense. But many are not truly independent. Politically and economically they remain no better than colonies. For a time their borders are respected. But then came new ideas about a globalised world, a world without borders. How can a country be independent if its borders are not sacred, if anyone can cross its borders freely and do anything he likes within the country?

Of course, globalisation is about free trade, open borders and free access. Countries should not protect their own banks and companies through discriminatory laws. Foreign companies should be accorded national status, i.e., there should be no difference in the treatment of local businesses and foreign-owned businesses. This, it is claimed, will benefit the developing countries and the consumers. They would have access to the best services and products at the lowest prices.

But if the big foreign corporations operate freely in a country, would they not kill all the local companies? Would they not become so powerful that they would wield a disproportionately strong influence on local society and local politics? Would they not dominate the governments, as was the case with the so-called banana republics?

Historically the East India Companies set up by the European countries in order to trade with Asia ended up colonising the countries with which they traded. Thus India, Burma and Malaysia were made colonies of the British Empire while the Malay Archipelago became the Dutch East Indies.

History has a way of repeating itself. The giant corporations and banks which belong to the rich Western countries can behave like the East India Companies of the past. From merely demanding for unfettered trade, they can go on to dominate and control the governments of the countries which had been opened to them. The end result will not be much different from the colonisation which had followed trading by the European trading companies of the past. Then the struggle for independence can begin all over again and there could be violence and even a new series of wars of liberation.

Perhaps this is too pessimistic a picture of the future. But nothing that is happening today or in the aftermath of the two world wars is reassuring. While Europe has experienced a period of peace unprecedented in its history; while Europe has consolidated into the European Union (E.U.); while North America has continued to prosper, and to unite into one solid bloc, the developing countries continue to be developing. In East Asia, a few have managed to progress but suddenly attacks on their currencies have pushed back their economies by almost two decades.

Practically all the developing countries are indebted to the rich, either directly or through their agencies. They have to place themselves under the direction of the powerful countries. Although they try to conform to the norms determined by the rich, they find themselves quite unable to repay their debts. This means that their economies must be subjected to the directions of their creditor countries. In effect they have become debt slaves, having lost their rights to take charge of the administration and management of their economies.

The unfortunate thing is that the advice they are getting from the creditor countries and their agencies would keep them poor, unable to recover and unable to pay back their debts. It may not be intentional but few countries which had accepted the advice have been able to recover.

It must be remembered that the developed countries were once as poor and as backward as the developing countries of today. They had become developed by not doing what they are advising the developing countries to do now, i.e., by not being liberal, not opening up their borders; by protecting their young industries and by rigid regulations and laws devised by their governments. The assertion that from the very beginning they had practised free trade and open competition is not borne out by the facts of history. We know that their East India Companies thrived and prospered through monopolies, through divisions in their spheres of trading activities, through militarily defended trading stations and eventually through colonising the countries with which they were trading.

As for democracy, human rights, labour rights, justice and fair play, their colonies and trading partners experienced nothing of these. There was no way the colonies or the trading partners could get fair trading, i.e., fair and competitive prices for their products.

The British had a policy called Imperial Preference through which they and their products gained privileged access to land for estates, and markets for their goods within the British Empire. The Dutch had a system of forcing farmers to produce and sell their agricultural products to Dutch monopolies. Other countries used slaves or indentured labour to work on their estates.

Had there been a free press, freedom of speech, democratic elections and human rights, it is most unlikely that the exploitation of the wealth of the colonial countries and trading partners could have gone on for a sufficient length of time for the colonial powers to prosper.

The point that has to be made is that it is not democracy, free trade and good governance that made the developed countries what they are today. Yet we are being told that the way to develop developing countries is to embrace globalisation and a borderless world, to deregulate, to do away with protectionism, to be democratic and to be liberal. From what we have seen and experienced, the mere floating of our currencies can already lead to financial and economic disaster. Many countries are practically without effective government because of the democratic processes. How do our puny banks and corporations compete against the super giants which have been formed in order to take advantage of a borderless world?

Today in addition to the economic woes resulting from attempts to standardise practices in a globalised world, we are all also assailed by fears of terror attacks.

Terrorism has always been with us. In the two world wars, millions of non-combatants died and millions more maimed for life. One cannot say they were not terrified by the wars. Since then many people in many places have suffered from terror attacks. But they are not of the rich and the strong. They are quite ordinary citizens of rather inconsequential countries. Two hundred thousand Bosnians died from Serbian ethnic cleansing. Palestinians and Israelis died also. So do the Chechens, the Kashmiris, the Rwandans, the Watutsies, the Chileans and the Argentines. But the world was not moved to wage a world war on terrorists because these unimportant people have been terrorised.

Then on September 11, 2001, the World Trade Center in New York, the business capital of the richest and most powerful nation of the world, was attacked. And everyone realised that no one is safe. The world united to fight against global terrorism.

Unfortunately, the world has never handled global terrorism of this kind. We think in terms of conventional warfare. We think if we can defeat them militarily they would surrender and sue for peace.

And so billions and billions of dollars are spent on upgrading defence and security. The only result is to harass ourselves and make us all live in constant fear of being the next victim of terror attacks. We fear flying, we fear travelling, we fear certain countries, we fear certain religions, we fear certain people, we fear the shoes they wear, we fear cargo ships, imported goods, letters and parcels—in fact, we fear everything around us. And because of these fears we no longer invest in our own countries or in foreign countries. And the economy of the world, the economy of every country, regresses and fails.

Actually the perpetrators of the September 11 attacks and the al-Qa'eda cannot possibly expect such a result from their attacks. They have really shaken the whole world and it looks like we are going to feel this fear and the consequences for a very long time.

The success of the September 11 attacks is due much more to our wrong handling of the situation than the extent of the actual damage done. The billions being lost by the whole world today through economic recession, the billions being spent on security and defence, can build hundreds of World Trade Center towers.

The Israelis should know by now that defence and security measures and even out-terrorising the terrorists have not stopped the suicide bombers. The world is far less thorough in defence and security than the Israelis. It stands to reason that the world's fight against terror through the upgrading of defence and security measures is going to be far less successful than the Israelis.

We may not want to admit it but the terrorists are not terrorising for the fun of it. They have a reason. We may think that their reason does not warrant the kind of actions they are taking. But that kind of thinking on our part is not going to get us anywhere. We have to look into what motivates them. If we care to look and acknowledge the causes leading to their acts of terror and try to remove them, then we may be able to at least reduce such acts from occurring.

There are many causes and because we will not be able to attend to all of them we cannot stop terrorism completely. But I would like to insist that the principle reason is territorial and not religious. The Palestinians have had their land taken away from them and they have been expelled from their land and made refugees. Every time they try to regain their land, they lost even more. Their struggle has been ignored by the world. Even the killings of their people, children and non-combatants included, raised hardly an eyebrow. Unable to wage conventional war, they resort to acts of terror.

Although friendly Muslim countries are unable to help the Palestinians, the people of these countries do not feel that they should be bound by the policies of their government. And so we find Muslims from other parts of the world taking part in these acts of terror.

From among the more than a billion Muslims there must be several thousands who would be willing to lose their lives in what they believe is a struggle for justice. We have to acknowledge this fact if we are to succeed in stopping global terrorism.

But, unfortunately, the world is merely aggravating the situation. Not only are we not trying to remove the causes, we are actually creating new ones. There was a time when Muslim countries were in agreement over the need to stop Iraqi aggressiveness. Today, that unity of purpose has disappeared. Muslims see the stance taken against Iraq as another act of discrimination against Muslims.

If Iraq is attacked not only will it be a distraction in the fight against global terrorism but it is likely to increase the number of recruits to the ranks of terrorists.

Iraq, Iran and North Korea have been labelled as the "axis of evil". But despite the fact that North Korea has admitted that it has nuclear capability it is not being threatened with war as Iraq is.

We do not want to see North Korea being threatened with war and the country being militarily attacked but the accommodating attitude towards North Korea is going to anger Muslims even more. Yet when North Korea agreed to cooperate and end its nuclear programme, it had not been appreciated. There was no relaxation of the condemnation of North Korea nor had food and other aid been given. Justified or not,

North Korea feels it had been let down. Hence the more uncooperative and belligerent attitude that it adopted recently.

North Korea has never been an easy country to deal with. But whether it joins the world community or not, it is still a part of our Global Village. We have to learn how to befriend it and get its cooperation. Cutting off supplies of food and other necessities will not bring it to its knees. Perhaps we can nuclear bomb it out of existence. But that would be a confession of our failure.

Looking at Iraq, North Korea, Palestine and many other hot spots, I cannot help feeling that despite all our technological progress, our claim to have established a modern, more humane and sophisticated civilisation, I cannot help feeling that we have failed to learn how to cope, how to manage the world. We still think in terms of the capacity to kill as the determinant of our strength. We still think that might is right, that the strong must dominate and the weak must submit.

Frankly, I do not think we have progressed much from the Stone Age. They used clubs and we use nuclear weapons, but the promise is still the same.

It is time we pause and rethink. Labelling people as "Satan" or belonging to the "axis of evil" merely provoke but does not resolve anything. Oppressing people or destroying their countries will not solve problems either. We have to get away from our old culture and values and reinvent our civilisation. The globalised world needs a change in our perception of things and in our way of dealing with the problems that must arise with change.

We cannot live in isolation any more. Globalisation is not about trade and investment only. Globalisation must affect everything that we do. We must also accept the fact that nothing happens in one part of the world without repercussions on the rest. The attack on the World Trade Center on September 11 is not an attack on the U.S. alone. It is an attack on the whole world. By the same token, the dispossession of Palestinian land is not an exclusive problem of the Palestinians. The terrorism that assails the world today has a direct connection with the fate of the Palestinians. Terror has become as globalised as trade and investment. The law and policymakers of the world cannot limit their interest to their countries alone. They have to be interested in the whole world. That is why it is useful for them to come together and discuss their national problems as international issues, as problems which affect the whole world.

5

Islam condemns acts of terror

"But Muslims everywhere must condemn terrorism once it is clearly defined. Terrorising people is not the way of Islam. Certainly killing innocent people is not Islamic."

TERRORISM, as we all know, has always been with us. It is not a new phenomenon. What is new is that newer and more diabolical ways have been used in order to kill and injure more people and achieve more spectacular damage.

A speech delivered at the Extraordinary Session of the Islamic Conference of Foreign Ministers on Terrorism in Kuala Lumpur, Malaysia, on April 1, 2002

But we have always been ambiguous regarding terrorism in other countries as not really terrorism but as the legitimate struggles of people against their oppressive governments or alien rule. As long as it happens to other people we do not believe we should do anything.

Certainly we do not feel a need for a universal effort to fight against terrorism.

But we know now that no country is safe, no one is safe.

We recognise now that terrorism is a crime, a heinous crime against humanity as a whole. It is a crime against the whole world no matter who, what or which country has been or is being targeted. The attacks of September 11 affects the whole world and damages not just buildings in a particular country and the people in them but it has struck at the very foundation of the world's economy and it has resulted in death and destruction for the country and people believed to be the base of the attacks. It has shattered the confidence of the world and has left an atmosphere of fear. The fallout from that terror attack is not over yet. Others will suffer, will lose their freedom, their rights and will lose their lives too. They will have to flee from their countries and live in misery in subhuman conditions.

Even the richest and most powerful countries, far removed from the scene of terror attacks will pay the price in other ways.

Perhaps the September 11 attacks are unusual in the extent of the fallout. But terror attacks in the past have also had an effect on the world. We may not have realised it but actually for years now we have been living in fear. That is why we accept the security measures taken by every country. We know that even the innocent among us may be gunned down, or kidnapped and killed.

There was a time when air travel was so safe that nobody checked our luggage. Then came the first hijacking. Since then we have to undergo ever more stringent checks, ever more inconveniences. And yet we still feel fear, for despite the checks the aircrafts could still be used as guided missiles even. We will be stricter now, but we can never really be certain that the aircraft we are travelling in would not be exposed to newer acts of terror. We fly despite the inconvenience of security checks but we fly in fear.

Millions of us need to travel and whether we are in the air or on the ground we will always be exposed to terror attacks, to kidnapping, being held to ransom and killed even.

The world is inventing more and more new weapons for conventional war. Every country prepares for a frontal attack. And so the weapons race goes on, bleeding the nations involved, bleeding other nations as they are forced to acquire these weapons which they will never use for decades.

But all the while there will be some people, misguided perhaps, who watch the development of these weapons. These are the people who plan to make terror attacks. And there will be any number of greedy people willing to procure and sell the latest weaponry to would-be terrorists.

Today, it is entirely possible for terrorists to acquire weapons of mass destruction. A small vial of deadly bacteria or virus is not too difficult to come by. Indeed it is possible now to acquire nuclear weapons even. Whether the world is aware of it or not we are being held to ransom. We pay a high price for protection but some day, despite all our precautions and security arrangements, we may see these weapons being employed not by security forces but by terror groups or individuals.

And all this while the cost of defense against terrorism will mount inexorably, both in terms of money and our convenience and our lifestyle.

We must all fight against terrorists and terrorism for none of us are really safe. But we cannot fight an enemy we cannot identify.

Fighting terrorists is not like fighting another country. We can flatten the enemy country until nothing is left of that country. It is entirely possible to do that now, and it has been done. But we can still miss the terrorists, for we do not know who they are and where they are. They may not be in the country we have destroyed. They may be elsewhere; they may even be in our own country.

Today, people are mobile and there is no country that is ethnically pure. Migration takes place as travel becomes easier and almost every country will become ever more multiracial, multireligious and multiethnic. Swearing allegiance guarantees nothing. There will always be aliens among us. We cannot keep track of all the aliens in all the countries. In fact, we can never be certain that our own people might not be terrorists or potential terrorists.

We cannot hunt down terrorists until we all agree who they are and we cooperate in the hunt. We have a need to agree on the way to identify the terrorist, to agree on what constitutes an act of terror. Discriminating against people who are ethnically or religiously similar to the terrorists only angers more people and perhaps contribute to the breeding of new terrorists. It is counter-productive.

We already know that it is entirely possible for freedom fighters struggling against oppression to be mistaken for and to be deliberately labelled as terrorists by their oppressors. Thus Jomo Kenyatta, Robert Mugabe, Nelson Mandela and Sam Nujoma were all labelled as terrorists, were hunted and faced jail sentences if they were captured.

But we know that today they are accepted as respected leaders of their countries.

Clearly, today's terrorists may be redesignated freedom fighters tomorrow and today's freedom fighters may become terrorists the next day depending on circumstances. If we hunt everyone whom some people refer to as terrorists we may be doing a great deal of injustice.

On the other hand, misguided people and countries may harbour and support terrorists believing them to be fighting for a legitimate cause. In the liberal Western countries there are quite a few terrorist cells working in support of terrorist organisations in other countries. They are not too different from Afghanistan which provided a haven for the al-Qa'eda terrorists.

So how do we identify terrorists? How do we distinguish freedom fighters from terrorists? How do we determine which government should be condemned for acts of terrorism or harbouring terrorists?

War is about killing people. Why should it matter how people are killed? Yet today in war poison gas is outlawed by international convention. In the struggles waged by oppressed people, can there be weapons or forms of attacks, which should be proscribed by international convention? Can there be aggressive acts by those in authority, which should be condemned and punished?

Terrorists will not respect convention. So what good would conventions do in the fight against terrorists? Nothing at all. But it will put the onus on governments everywhere to act against those who violate these conventions.

Before we can agree on the conventions we must decide what acts constitute acts of terror and who should be described as terrorists.

I would like to suggest here that armed attacks or other forms of attack against civilians must be regarded as acts of terror and the perpetrators regarded as terrorists. Whether the attackers are acting on their own or on the orders of their governments, whether they are regulars or irregulars, if the attack is against civilians, then they must be considered as terrorists.

Groups or governments which support attacks on civilians must be regarded as terrorists, irrespective of the justification of the operations carried out, irrespective of the nobility of the struggle.

However, if civilians are accidentally caught in the crossfire, the attackers should not be labelled as terrorists.

According to this definition of terrorism, the attack on the World Trade Center on September 11, the human bomb attacks by Palestinians and the Tamil Tigers, the attacks against civilians by Israeli forces, the killings of Bosnian Muslims and others must be considered as acts of terror and the perpetrators must be condemned as terrorists. And anyone supporting them must be considered as terrorists, too. Where states are behind the acts of terrorism, the whole government must stand condemned. But no race or religion should be condemned or discriminated against simply because people of the same race or their co-religionists have been involved in terrorist activities.

While we may be able to agree on what constitute acts of terrorism and who should be condemned as terrorists, it is important that there is international agreement on the condemnation of any particular incident or incidents as acts of terror by terrorists. Then the world community can cooperate and participate in whatever action is to be taken against the perpetrators. Here, there is no authority more competent than the U.N. to make these decisions. Once the U.N. has decided, the whole world must cooperate fully in the fight against the terrorists concerned.

While we should identify terrorists everywhere and act in whatever way prescribed, we must also find ways and means to prevent as much as possible the tendency of certain people or governments to resort to terrorism. We must identify the causes of their bitterness and anger and we must remove these causes. I don't think people would want to blast themselves to death simply because they enjoy doing so. These are acts of the desperate, acts of people who see no way of redressing their grievances, of alleviating their sufferings. We cannot just dismiss them as senseless perverts who enjoy terrorising people.

If we want to stop new acts of terrorism we will have to attend to the causes of the bitterness and anger and try to eliminate them. We must seriously try to do this.

Today, we live in a glaringly inequitable world. While some countries and people are terribly rich and powerful, other countries are terribly poor. Even within countries, there is extreme disparity in the wealth of the rich and poor. Today, capitalism is supreme and there is no more option to defect to the Socialist or the communist system. The rich of today do not even try to hide their avarice and acquisitiveness. In fact, in the eyes of the helplessly poor, the rich appear very oppressive, forcing them to accept systems, ideologies and values which they are not yet ready for. Worldwide, there is a great deal of bitterness and anger among the deprived because of the resulting disparities between the rich and poor, the strong and weak. These factors can lead to acts of terror.

The world must address these injustices more seriously than just preaching the values of tolerance and understanding while ignoring the adverse results of these "virtues".

For the Muslims the grievances are real and truly unbearable, beyond mere understanding and tolerance. For the past five decades, the Palestinians, for example, have not only had their lands confiscated, they had also been expelled from their own land by the Israelis. Their puny attempts to regain their territory through conventional war with the help of friendly states failed and they lost more land. In the occupied land, the Palestinians were subjected to oppression and humiliation. Because they throw stone at the Israelis they are shot at and killed, children included. For the Israelis, it is not an eye for an eye; it is a life for being hit by a stone. They believe that by terrorising the terrorists they can stop the carnage. The suicide bombers consider themselves already dead and are on their way to heaven. They are not likely to be deterred by the threat of death. Killing their leader is not going to help either. More violent leaders will replace the fallen leader and the terror attacks will go on. The Holocaust did not defeat the Jews. A second Holocaust with Arabs for victims will not defeat the Arabs either. The Israelis must come to their senses and opt for deescalation of terror rather than escalating it.

If the Israelis won't, then the world must forcibly stop them. If we are serious about stopping terrorists, then we must stop both the Palestinians and the Israelis from mutual massacre.

In Bosnia-Herzegovina, more than a hundred thousand Muslims were massacred in full view of television viewers and for a long time nothing was done. The Muslims were actually prevented from acquiring weapons to defend themselves because this might result in more killings, i.e., the death of their enemies might add to the number of casualties. If only Muslims were killed and the Serbs saved then obviously the casualties would be less. We have seen that the world can put a stop to the killings of Muslims, but the world acted very late. Yet the Slovenes and the Croats could be protected and they were able to gain their independence without too much bloodshed.

Elsewhere Muslim countries are subjected to attacks and economic sanctions resulting in many deaths from deprivations of all kinds.

Because of all these there is a great deal of bitterness and anger among Muslims. The impotence of Muslim countries to do anything to remedy the situation adds to this frustration and anger. While the majority of them are resigned to their fate, a small number cannot help but feel a need to vent their anger in some way.

These people may be misguided. They may be wrong in believing they are fighting a *jihad*, a holy war. They may achieve nothing to put an end to their grievances. Indeed, they may actually be doing a lot of harm to their cause, to their co-religionists, to Islam itself. But the fact remains that they are very angry and bitter and willing to commit terrible acts of terror, even if they lose their lives in the process.

The world must deal with these misguided people not just by hunting them down but also by removing the causes of their anger and frustration.

In Malaysia, we had to deal with terrorists for 42 long years—from 1948 to 1990. We fought against them, we hunted them and we punished them. But we also looked into the causes of their insurrection. We found that they were mainly Chinese who felt alienated because they had not been given citizenship status by the British. Their insurrection was supported by the majority of ordinary Chinese who sympathised with them and who also felt just as alienated.

Accordingly, the independent Malaysian government gave more than a million citizenship to the Chinese, protected them, provided land for them, enabled them to go about their business, and gave them a meaningful participation in the government of the country. This was what the Malaysian government refers to as winning the hearts and minds of the people. And the Chinese were won over. They slowly ceased helping the terrorists, stopped the recruitment of new members and they actually helped the government apprehend many of them.

What the government did may sound like appeasement. It may encourage people to resort to terrorism in order to achieve their objectives. But by removing their grievances and the causes of their violent anger, they had to admit that their struggle had become meaningless. Eventually they laid down arms. Today, Malaysians of Chinese origin are peace-loving people and are loyal to the country.

If Malaysia's experience is anything to go by, in the fight against terrorism worldwide, the causes, the grievances of the terrorists, must be attended to. We must win the hearts and minds of the people most likely to support or resort to terrorism.

The extreme disparity between rich and poor and poverty must be reduced, the rigid insistence that everyone must accept the same ideology and set of values must be relaxed and in the case of the Muslims, the oppression of the Palestinians and the other Muslims and their countries must be brought to an end.

But Muslims everywhere must condemn terrorism once it is clearly defined. Terrorising people is not the way of Islam. Certainly killing innocent people is not Islamic. Bitter and angry though we may be, we must demonstrate to the world that Muslims are rational people when fighting for our rights and we do not resort to acts of terror. We must object strongly to the linking of Muslims with terror just because a few Muslims have resorted to acts of terror. We must point out that Christians, Buddhists, Hindus, Jews and others are equally guilty of terrorism. Terrorists must be identified by their acts, and nothing else. And we as responsible Muslims must contribute to the fight against terrorism by helping to define what constitutes terrorism and who the terrorists are. And when that is done we can all join in the fight against the terrorists, be they Muslims, Christians, Hindus or Jews.

The September 11 attacks on New York and Washington, D.C. are unmitigated disaster for Muslims all over the world. Our image, which had not been good, has been made worse. It does not help that we are all weak and disunited.

If the present crises in the Muslim world are to be overcome we have to be serious about handling it. You are here, I believe, because you recognise the danger facing us. Unless we are able to turn the present worldwide anger over the terror attacks of September 11 into a real campaign against all terrorists, irrespective of their religious faiths, we are going to find that Muslim bashing will be heightened and our struggle to alleviate the sufferings of hundreds of millions of oppressed Muslims will fail.

We have a duty here to the Muslim *ummah*, to Islam and to Allah. Let us put aside other considerations and strive for consensus in our fight against the blight of blind anger and frustration and prove that Islam is indeed a way of life that will bring about well-being and glory to Muslims and to Mankind as a whole.

6

Malaysia has no tolerance for terrorists

"Fighting against terrorists is not like fighting against a country. You can defeat a country and end the war with a military victory. But terrorists do not operate from within a country. They can be anywhere. They can be anybody. They can act in concert or alone."

THE United States and Malaysia have many things in common, much more than most people realise. We share a common history, language, many of our values, goals and even challenges. It is appropriate, therefore, that our two flags should be so much alike that, many mistake one for the other.

A speech delivered at the U.S.-Asean Business Council Dinner in Washington, D.C., United States, on May 14, 2002

To begin with, we both achieved independence from the same colonial power, from whom we inherited the same language, common law system, and principles of representative government. What you may not know is that America's success in freeing itself from British rule led directly to the colonisation of what is now Malaysia, by the very same colonialists. In 1786, only five years after the Continental Army led by General George Washington defeated the British at Yorktown, the same British commander who surrendered to Washington, Lord Cornwallis acquired what is now the state of Penang, as a British colony. Thus began the British colonisation of the Malay states.

The American Revolution had an even more profound impact on Malaysia, however. The founding fathers of this country—Jefferson, Madison, Franklin, Adams and others—gave Malaysia its model of governance based on regular, democratic elections, separation of powers, and the protection of fundamental civil liberties.

America's welcome mat for the oppressed people of other countries has made it a melting-pot of multiethnicity and multiculturalism upon which you built a prosperous, powerful and forward-looking nation. Malaysia too attracted immigrants to our shores. And today our people is made up of indigenous Malays, descendants of Chinese, Indians and other migrants, living together in peace and a climate of tolerance and mutual respect. Our diversity, like yours, is the basis of our strength.

With all of this in common, it is natural that we should see eye to eye on many things affecting us and the world. Besides, some 150,000 Malaysians lived and studied here and are now helping to shape the mores and policies of the country.

Since Malaysia's industrialisation the U.S. has become Malaysia's largest trading partner and export destination. In 2001, the U.S. accounted for 18.3 per cent of Malaysia's global trade, 20.2 per cent of exports and 16 per cent of imports. Total trade with the U.S. in 2001 amounted to US$29.6 billion with exports valued at US$17.8 billion and imports US$11.8 billion, most of which is made up of manufactured goods.

While 75.3 per cent of Malaysia's total exports to the U.S. is made up of electrical and electronic products, we also export textiles and apparels, optical and scientific products and rubber products to the U.S.

U.S. investment in Malaysia have been growing consistently and the U.S. remains the largest source of foreign direct investment (FDI), both cumulatively and on an annual basis, over the last few years. Cumulative U.S. investment amounted to US$10.5 billion in 2001, mainly in manufacturing, petroleum-related and service-based industries. U.S. investment are particularly significant in the electrical and electronics industry. More than 30 of the *Fortune 500* companies have operations in Malaysia. Among them are Intel, Motorola, Dell, Agilent, Dow Chemicals, Exxon Mobil, Hewlett-Packard, Solectron and Goodyear. U.S. companies are comfortable in Malaysia, where the business climate is safe, secure and very positive and profit—especially for U.S. companies—have been exceptionally high. We do not begrudge you this. To us profit is not a sin and you are welcome to it.

Malaysia has continued to attract a significant amount of FDI despite the intense competition for FDI worldwide. Foreign investment in the manufacturing sector over the five-year period between 1997 and 2001 amounted to US$19.7 billion and accounted for over 58 per cent of total approved investments. The major sources of FDI were from the U.S., Japan, the E.U., Singapore and Taiwan.

The U.S. and Malaysia have also faced—and continue to face—common challenges. During the post-World War II era, the U.S. confronted the challenge of an expansionistic communism. For over 42 years, Malaysia fought against militant communism which we eventually defeated, at a great cost in blood and resources.

Today, militant communism is no longer a threat. But, we now face another common threat, which constitutes a greater challenge—terrorism. Terrorism is a crime, a crime against humanity as a whole. It is a crime against the whole world no matter who, what or which country has been or is being targeted. The attacks on September 11 affect the whole world and damages not just buildings in a particular country and the people in them. It has shattered the confidence of the world and has left an atmosphere of fear.

Let me be perfectly clear about one thing. Malaysia has no tolerance for terrorists. Whether people are fighting for what they consider a noble cause or not, there are certain acts which they may not perpetrate. Detonating bombs in public places and killing innocent civilians cannot be accepted. Holding people to ransom or as shields cannot be accepted. Poisoning food, medicine or water supply cannot be accepted. Deliberate killing of civilians even when sanctioned by legitimate governments is equally unacceptable. These are acts of terror and anyone committing these acts must be regarded as terrorists by everyone irrespective of the causes they are fighting for, irrespective of their religion, race or creed. And once they are defined as terrorists, it is the duty of everyone, every country, to hunt them down and bring them to justice. There must be no discrimination on any basis.

The attack on the World Trade Center on September 11, the human bomb attacks by Palestinians and the Tamil Tigers, the attacks against civilians by Israeli forces, in Jenin and elsewhere, the killings of Bosnian Muslims and others are all acts of terrorism and the perpetrators must therefore be condemned as terrorists. Where states are behind the acts of terrorism, their governments must stand condemned. But no race or religion should be condemned or discriminated against simply because people of the same race or their co-religionists have been involved in terrorist activities.

In Malaysia, we have been very successful in our own fight against terrorism. The communist insurgents whom we defeated practised widespread terrorism. We defeated them, and eradicated terrorism from our country not only by military means, but also by addressing the root causes of the terrorism that plagued Malaysia. Terrorism can never be justified, under any circumstances. However, if we are to prevent it, we must not only hunt down all the terrorists but also remove the root causes that make some people angry and bitter enough to commit or support acts of terror. By addressing the grievances of our Chinese community, from which most of the terrorists sprang, we were able to put an end to terrorism in Malaysia.

Recently, Malaysia had to deal with another source of terrorism: extremist Muslim groups who claim that our government is not Islamic and want to replace it with a Taliban-style state spanning Malaysia, Indonesia and the southern Philippines. They are opposed by the overwhelming majority of Malaysians, including Muslim Malaysians, who want to preserve our democratic, multireligious, multiethnic and multicultural society and the spirit of religious and ethnic tolerance that underlies it. We Malaysians want to preserve our commitment to modernisation, development and openness to the outside world, which have played such an important role in our unprecedented economic growth and prosperity over the past two decades.

We studied the causes of extremism among Muslims and why they resort to terror but found that they were misled by the situation in other Islamic countries and their wrong perceptions of Islam. We have taken measures to ensure the spread of the true teachings of Islam as espoused by the majority of Malaysian Muslims. Fundamental Islam proscribes suicides and the killing of innocent people and Muslims should not resort to indiscriminate violence, but should seek peace instead. As to the situations in other Muslim countries, in Palestine, for example, we will try to alleviate them, to help overcome their problems. Accordingly, we have been able to act against would-be terrorists in accordance with our laws with the full support of our people.

We are firm when dealing with terrorists, whether they are Chinese, Indians or Malays, Muslims or non-Muslims. If anyone plots terror in Malaysia he will be arrested under the laws of the country. As one of your newsmagazines recently wrote, Kuala Lumpur is a modern and attractive city, an outstanding place to do business, but also to rest and relax. But this is not so for terrorists. We do not tolerate their presence. We give them no rest, no quarter, and no place to hide. We have adequate laws and capacity to deal with such threats. And we have had much experience in this field.

Malaysia is willing to support neighbouring countries within Asean, the international community, and the U.S. in the fight against terrorism. Long before September 11 we have shared information with the U.S. and acted against suspected terrorists.

We are still doing so with regard to suspected al-Qa'eda members. If they are Malaysians then we take action against them ourselves and this includes putting them back on the right path.

President George W. Bush has acknowledged Malaysia's support in the fight against terrorism. He expressed these sentiments in both of our face-to-face meetings, in Shanghai last October, and again today at the White House. We see eye to eye on this important issue of terrorism and that the U.S. can count on Malaysia's continued support in the fight against terrorism.

Thus far, I have talked about what the U.S. and Malaysia have in common. There is certainly a lot. But we also have important differences. Malaysia is, as you know, a Muslim-majority state. Unfortunately, many people in the West unthinkingly and disparagingly identify Muslims with terrorism. This is not only wrong, it is counter-productive. Discriminating against people who are ethnically or religiously similar to the terrorists only angers more people and perhaps contributes to the breeding of new terrorists.

Muslims do have serious grievances. The Palestinians in the occupied territories are subjected to oppression and humiliation. Israeli troops attack and kill Palestinian civilians, including women and children, who have nothing to do with suicide bombers; they bulldoze their homes and demolish their businesses; they destroy airports, water and electricity supply. In Bosnia-Herzegovina, more than a hundred thousand Muslims were massacred in full sight of television viewers and for a long time nothing was done.

Elsewhere Muslim countries are subjected to attacks and economic sanctions resulting in many deaths from deprivations of all kinds. Because of all these there is a great deal of bitterness and anger among Muslims.

We would like to see Muslims and their countries express their anger and frustrations in a rational way. They should defend themselves with conventional methods. By and large, they do or try to do. But when these are futile, invariably there will be elements who cannot contain their anger and who resort to unacceptable ways not so much to prevent their own humiliation and oppression but merely to vent their anger and frustrations. While we must never excuse them for their counter-productive acts, we must nevertheless try to defuse their anger and the causes for it. I am afraid the world is not doing this. Indeed, with the events in Palestine, with Jenin, the anger has become worse. The fight against terrorists who are Muslims will therefore take longer. Fighting against terrorists is not like fighting against a country. You can defeat a country and end the war with a military victory. But terrorists do not operate from within a country. They can be anywhere. They can be anybody. They can act in concert or alone. They can destroy buildings or kidnap, snipe or kill individuals, individuals who may be completely innocent. The technique of fighting terrorists cannot be the same as fighting a country. It has to be different. Our view is that we must also remove the causes of their bitterness and anger.

Islam, in its true essence, is a religion of peace, tolerance, and respect for human life in all its variations. When it is properly understood, and its true precepts are followed, it offers a path to enlightenment, to harmony, to stable and responsible government, to progress and to prosperity. Malaysia is an Islamic state.

At the same time, and without contradiction, it is democratic, diverse, tolerant, peaceful, economically and politically stable, progressive and forward looking. There is no inherent conflict between Islam and any of these achievements. In fact, we believe that the way we adhere to the essential or fundamental teachings and practice of Islam in Malaysia has contributed to our success as a nation. We see no contradiction between Islam and women's equality, for example.

7

Making the world safe again

"The world must be made safe again. The world can be made safe if, instead of subscribing to the idea that terror can be fought with terror, indeed that terror can be fought with greater terror, we revert to achieving greater understanding between people and to the building of friendship between them."

THE tragic events of September 11 has shocked all of us into realising that no one is truly safe and that borders and distances are no longer the protective wall that we believe them to be. Technology has advanced and along with the good things that it brings must come the negative, the abuses which will

---

A speech delivered at the meeting of the U.S. Congress' Malaysia-America Friendship Caucus at Capitol Hill, Washington, D.C., United States, on May 14, 2002

force us to rethink the things that we had welcome with so much joy and expectations. At the same time we must realise that globalisation is not just about economic and business opportunities, of greater possibilities of making more and more money. It is also about better communication and faster travel for those who are bent on doing harm to those whom they may consider as their enemies; even to those who are innocent who may be made the victim of the vengeful, the callous and the anarchic.

As much as we must get the whole world to agree to universal systems for international relations and business, we must also get the whole world to cooperate in fighting those who abuse the new internationalism. In fighting against the terrorists we must agree to act together and play our part.

We may not like to acknowledge it, but the world is now living in fear. We had happily taken to the air, flitting from place to place, as if we are visiting friends across the street, or across town. But we no longer feel safe even if we fly a short distance. We cannot even be sure that innocent though we may be, we will not be the target and the victims of terror attacks as we go about our work or as we enjoy leisure in our own country or outside. The world may not think much of one life lost, but if it is our life which is lost, we have lost everything.

We have to prevent this from happening. The world must be made safe again. The world can be made safe if, instead of subscribing to the idea that terror can be fought with terror, indeed that terror can be fought with greater terror, we revert to achieving greater understanding between people and to the building of friendship between them.

The U.S. and Americans were the most liked people not so long ago. In Malaysia, we were grateful to

America because we were liberated from Japanese occupation by Americans largely. Americans were our heroes and our friends. The first person to condemn British colonisation of the Malay states was Rupert Emerson, an American professor. He wrote his book, *Malaysia: A Study in Direct and Indirect Rule* (1937), before World War II, long before we called our country "Malaysia"; at a time when we were known to the world as "Malaya". He was omniscient. He foresaw Malaysia before we even thought about independence and the unification of the Malay states into Malaysia.

After our independence in 1957 we welcomed the American Peace Corp. They did immense work to seal the friendship between Malaysians and indeed the peoples of other developing countries with America. The U.S. became the best friend of the colonial people seeking independence and their friend and guide after independence. The U.S. gladly gave independence to the Philippines.

America and the American people were the best friends of all the oppressed people of the world. But America also remained the best friend of the Europeans as the Marshall Plan made economic recovery possible for the European countries. Clearly America was the best friend of the world. In the confrontations between the communist bloc and the Western bloc few had any difficulty in choosing America and the West.

When the confrontation ended with the defeat of the communist bloc the world saw a period of world peace and unprecedented prosperity. The world even welcomed the role of the U.S. as the policeman, the law keeper of the world.

I would be lying if I say that the world still see the U.S. as the friend that they knew. Yet there is every reason and every possibility for the U.S. and the

Americans to be once again the universal friend of the world. All that is needed is to be more gentle when faced with recalcitrant nations and people. People tend to respond more positively to the friendly approach than to confrontations. Pushed into a corner, even the weakest will fight. Victory over them will really not mean much.

A Malaysian was asked by the United Nations to persuade Burma to be democratic and more conciliatory towards Aung San Suu Kyi. Persuasion must take time. We think we are making progress. The Malaysian government has not been asked to do anything but we try to help Burma make the transition by assuring the military government leaders that they will not end in jail if they opt for democracy.

One must remember that when Ershad of Bangladesh and Chun Doo-hwan were persuaded to accept democracy, they both ended up in jail, Chun Doo-hwan being sentenced to death. The fate of Suharto is not encouraging either for dictators to give up power in favour of democracy.

To cut a long story short, the Burmese junta is now less resistant towards a switch to democracy. They have released a substantial number of their political prisoners. It is not easy for them. Already attempts are being made to topple the junta. They have to be careful if they want to stay in power to make the transition.

The West is very impatient. You want an overnight change. Sudden change, even if it is for the good, is disruptive. Democracy for people who are not used to it can undermine stability, resulting in war even. Sadly it does not compare well with the safety and stability achieved by an authoritarian society. So let there be patience. The loss in time is made up by the gain in the smoothness of the transition. It is important to remember that democracy is only a means and not an end in itself. It is the good life that democracy brings that counts, not democracy *per se*.

We in Malaysia understand Americans' anxiety to see that the freedom that they enjoy should be enjoyed also by Malaysians and other people. But we must admit that at the moment we are unable to accept the absolute freedom that you believe in. There are certain freedoms that you enjoy which we think we can do without. We hope you can tolerate our different sense of values. One day perhaps we will be comfortable with your values. But for the moment we are not comfortable. Let us celebrate the difference for that is what makes the world interesting.

If we can accept that there will always be differences between us, differences in culture, values and opinions, then we will be more tolerant of each other. Then we will be able to live in peace and friendship with each other. As you know, three very different people live in Malaysia. Apart from ethnic differences, we differ in religious beliefs, languages and cultures. Despite all these differences, we can live together, work together and play together. Not many multiethnic countries are able to enjoy peace, harmony and development. We are able to, because we accept the differences between us.

I am not trying to hold Malaysia up as a shining example to the world. But you will agree with me that being sensitive and tolerant helps peoples of different races, different countries to be at peace with each other. In fact, we can be great friends despite our differences. When the U.S. was young, you appreciated the recognition and support of whatever country, irrespective of their ethnic and religious differences. Moreover, an Arab Muslim country was among the first to recognise and cooperate with you. With the passage of time the whole world came to recognise and respect you. And you grew into the great country that you are today.

Today, you can afford to use your power and strength. But it would do you no harm to be friendly to other countries, to be patient with them and to win them over to your side.

8

The new threat of economic terrorism

"They [newly independent countries] are terrified of being colonised once again through economic pressure coupled with the propaganda of the media. They are being terrorised, terrorised in the same way that the terrorists are threatening the world."

IN the world today, nothing happens in one part of it which does not have repercussions on the rest. Whether we legislate into being globalisation or not, the interconnectivity of the world's economy is already a fact of life. Never was the interconnectivity of the world's economy better

---

A speech delivered at the Langkawi International Dialogue (LID) 2002 in Langkawi, Malaysia, on August 1, 2002

demonstrated than in the aftermath of the September 11 incident. The reaction of the international financial community and national economies was immediate. Bourses across Europe plummeted—the Paris exchange fell 7.4 per cent, the Frankfurt exchange 7 per cent and the London exchange 5.7 per cent. Speculations over retaliatory possibilities pushed crude oil prices up to a nine-month high. The economic effects were real and painful. The already shaky American economy began a steep downward slide. The East Asian electronics industry, already grappling with the problems of global overproduction, began to slide further and faster. And we have still not recovered.

The September 11 attack shocked the world. Many who thought terrorism was a problem of other countries now realise that no country is immune from terror attacks. Everyone now finds a need to cooperate to tackle this problem. Unfortunately, we cannot agree on how to deal with terrorists and terrorism. Some think that all that is needed is to declare war on terrorism and to mount a full military operation. Like fighting conventional war they see the terrorists being defeated and laying down their arms. There would be a victory parade and we would all go to bed feeling secure.

Unfortunately, fighting terrorists is not like fighting a conventional or civil war. In a conventional war, the enemy is a country, an alliance of countries, or a definable group. The object is to defeat the enemy by the ability to kill more people and do more damage. With terrorism there is no country which can be truly identified as the enemy. In fact, the terrorists may be hiding anywhere, or even be among the people of the country which is fighting against terrorism. Many of the terrorists may be killed or arrested but there is no guarantee there will be no more still around or new recruits deterred. And when the terrorists are prepared to kill themselves in carrying out their acts of terror, there is no way we can prevent them from doing that with any certainty.

If we really want to fight terrorism we must realise all these and we must have a strategy that takes into consideration the causes of terrorism. We must eliminate the causes even if they are silly and unreasonable if we want to win the hearts and minds of supporters and sympathisers and to prevail upon would-be terrorists to cease and desist. I am afraid this is not being done. In fact, the opposite is happening as terror attacks which are totally indiscriminate are being used to counter terrorism which have caused even more anger and desperation and more willingness on the part of the terrorists to respond in similar fashion.

The whole world, especially the world most likely to be attacked by terrorists, is living in a state of fear, expending hundreds of billions of dollars in futile defence and, in the process, preventing economic recovery.

While the rich fear the terrorists, the poor too are living in fear. They live in fear of the predatory rich bent upon taking over their economies and their countries. They fear their ultimate recolonisation.

What I say is not exaggeration or alarmist: globalisation and free trade along with democracy are being touted as the saviours of the world, of the poor in particular. But our experience up till now is that we are being destabilised and robbed.

The poor countries have always relied on the natural commodities they produce in order to export and earn foreign exchange with which to buy needed industrial goods. But we have seen how every year we have to sell more and more of our largely depleting resources in order to buy less and less of the goods we need. We are being held to ransom because the rich countries are not entirely dependent on us for the raw materials for their industry. They have a choice of sources and they control the market and the prices. They do not really care whether we buy their products or not because their markets are mainly they themselves, the rich countries.

Besides they invent and produce their own raw materials in order to compete with our natural products. Rubber is displaced by synthetics, tin by plastics, glass, paper, aluminium and numerous other packaging materials and now they have genetically modified products such as soya bean oil to oust palm oil from the market.

Genetic Modification (GM) is going to impoverish further the agro-wealth-based poor countries. Soya bean is a perfect example. By modifying the soya so as to produce more oil per hectare they are able to reduce their price to the same level as palm oil and other vegetable oils. While they themselves reject GM for health reasons they have no compunction about selling GM food to developing countries.

As if that is not enough they subsidise directly and indirectly all their farm products. While the World Bank and the International Monetary Fund (IMF) force many poor countries to stop subsidies, these agencies never stopped the rich from unfair and massive subsidies.

We are told to open up our economy to foreign participation. There is no doubt that FDI in industrial production creates jobs and increases the wealth of the poor. Malaysia has greatly benefited from FDI.

But now the rich are competing with the poor to attract FDI. They are providing land and capital free to foreign firms, including those from the nearly developing countries, to site their plants in the rich countries. And failure to set up plants in their countries can mean all kinds of non-tariff barriers (NTBs) and discrimination. The result is not an inflow of capital into the poor countries but starvation of FDI and even outflow of capital.

One rich country was able to attract a major investment away from Malaysia by offering US$200 million to the corporation apart from other perks. There is no way Malaysia can offer anything like this.

The Asian financial crisis of 1997 is another example of economic terrorism at work. The countries of East Asia were growing fast and were known as economic tigers prior to the crisis. South Korea was apparently going to become another Japan. The controlled Western media began to call South Korea a newly industrialising country (NIC). South Korea was very proud of this recognition. But it soon learnt that it was to justify all kinds of restrictions on the export of its products.

South Korea's labour practices and wages were scrutinised and condemned. The quality of its products was questioned and declared to be below the standards set up by the rich countries. Charges of dumping were levelled at South Korea and countervailing duties were applied to ensure that South Korean goods become uncompetitive. Still the South Korean growth continued and so did the other East Asian countries.

Timber products from Southeast Asia are boycotted because we are said to be destroying our forests. That Malaysia, for example, is 50 per cent covered by natural tropical forests, with 20 per cent more covered by tree estates, is ignored. They insist that we are destroying our forests.

Then the currency traders moved in loudly proclaiming that the economies of the East Asian countries were overheated and that their currencies were overvalued. The currency traders then sold these currencies in the market. It was a classic example of shortselling. They claimed they sold the currencies to avoid losses when the currencies devalued. But, in fact, they held none of the currencies. They merely sold short knowing that by doing so the currencies would be devalued. Then they expected to buy at the lower value to deliver the currency to the people who had bought earlier from them at a higher price. And they netted millions of dollars from this shortselling operation. And still they continued to sell and to devalue the currencies.

What happens when the currencies are devalued against the U.S. dollar? All trade is conducted in U.S. dollar. With devaluation, more local currency is needed to pay for imported goods. Suddenly the rich East Asian countries became poor. Malaysia needed twice the amount of ringgit in order to pay for imports. Indonesia had to pay six times the number of rupiahs for their imports. It was the same with Thailand, the Philippines, South Korea and even Taiwan. And because we could not find this much money we were not able to import and enjoy the same standard of living. In other words, we became poor.

At the same time, our economies collapsed. Millions were thrown out of work. People rioted, robbing and burning shophouses, blaming other citizens, killing them and raping the women. Politically and socially the countries became destabilised and law and order were unenforceable. Rebellion broke out. Attempts by law-enforcement authorities to restore respect for the law resulted in accusations of police brutality. The international electronic media covered the riots and showed repeatedly only police action and not the violence of the crowds.

The fall in the value of the currency undermined the stock markets. The dollar value of the shares plummeted. To save their investment, foreign investors began to sell and pull out their money. The market plunged further. Soon the banks accumulated huge non-performing loans (NPLs) and companies became insolvent. They could not get any credit to finance their operation. Many closed down and threw millions of employees to the streets.

And what did the currency traders and their media say? They claimed they were trying to discipline the governments. They claimed these Asian governments were all corrupt; they practise cronyism; they were not transparent; they did not practise good corporate governance. They, the currency traders, want to bring about more honesty in the governments and better practices in the economies of these Asian countries. They, the currency traders, are not to be blamed in any way for they merely wanted to see a better world. If they made money in the process it was incidental. Look, aren't they giving away their money to the poor? Aren't they great philanthropists?

They are, in fact, philanderers. They steal from the poor in order to give a minute fraction to the poor. They were trying to play Robin Hood but that hood stole from the rich to give to the poor. These modern hoods stole from the poor. And they have become billionaires. It is no big deal to give a minute amount of their ill-gotten gains to the poor. But their media made heroes of these daylight robbers whose depredations have resulted in the countries of East Asia remaining incapable of recovering to this day. Had there been no financial crisis the East Asian countries would become developed by now, able to match the economies of the Western nations.

Now we are being pressed to swallow globalisation and the free market. Globalisation, we are told, will bring about prosperity to the poor. This prosperity would come from allowing the big corporations of the world to invade our countries and do what they like. In the free market the most efficient corporations would win because they would have the ability to produce the best products and sell at the lowest prices. Free competition is what the free market is all about. Obviously the biggest corporations would win hands down. A level playing field is useless for the midgets and the weak. It will be the law of the jungle, the survival of the strongest. Might is going to be right even more than before.

And in confirmation of this, the giant corporations are busy merging and acquiring each other in order to become even bigger and stronger. There is near monopoly and certainly oligopoly in all the industries. With these hypergiants entering a small country there is no way that the little indigenous companies can survive. There will be no room for them. They will be wiped out, stamped underfoot like so many insects.

Governments will not be able to do anything as the free market is based on non-interference by the authorities. The market is supposed to regulate itself. In fact, these corporations will be so powerful that they will control not only the economy but also the politics of a country. We have seen how the countries of Central America have been controlled by the owners and managers of foreign-owned great banana plantations, to the point where they were described derisively as banana republics. The poor countries which become dependent on these huge foreign corporations upon globalisation will be controlled in the same way. There will be no choice for the people. There will be no democracy, despite all the talk about wanting us to be democratic.

We are told that these great corporations are so well administered that they will not just bring wealth to the poor but also ensure high standards of morality, of transparency by the native governments. Today we know that this is a joke. Look at the behaviour of some of the biggest corporations which were already well on the way to becoming world monopolies. They have no morality whatsoever. They cheat, they lie, they fiddle with their accounts and they are protected by their crony governments. A few have been exposed. We don't know how many more have been fiddling while the world's economy burns. Every week there is a new exposure.

And these are the people who are supposed to bring us prosperity, who are going to discipline us and ensure that we have high moral standards. It is a big laugh.

Unfortunately for us, it is not a laughing matter. Economic pressure is very real. The promotion of democracy may not be because democracy is good. It may be because democracy can destabilise us. I am all for democracy. It is the best system of governance ever devised by Man. But it does not always work. People must be sophisticated and must know the limits, if democracy is not to end up in anarchy. The great liberal democracies of the West have had some two hundred years of experience, of trials and errors and frequent abandonment of the system before it developed to the present state. In most of these countries there are only two effective political parties and one or the other can achieve majority and set up a government.

But the people in the new developing democracies only understand their rights and their freedom. For them, democracy means setting up political parties, any number of them in order to vie for political position. For them, freedom means saying anything against each other without regard to the sensitivities and consequences. For them, freedom means taking to the streets and rioting. For them freedom means breaking up the country to set up their own little states.

Where there are numerous parties, most of which are regional and not national, or they are extremely racial or tribal, majorities cannot be achieved in elections. Either minority governments or shaky coalitions have to be set up which are so preoccupied with trying to remain in power that the running of the country, the development of the country, is neglected. Corruption must of necessity be a feature as politicians try to make the most of their temporary power. Every time a new government is set up, the previous government leaders are accused of corruption, are hunted and jailed or deprived of their political rights. And the accusers become the accused when they in turn fall.

When governments are stable or remain in power for long, even if they are democratically elected and above-board they are accused of being undemocratic. The international media and the governments of the liberal countries will all work hard to undermine these countries. They cannot bring themselves to believe that the people want it this way. They cannot believe that the natives they had ruled before understand democracy or the rule of law. If they are stable and doing well then they must be dictators. They fabricate stories that although the people support the leaders of these countries enthusiastically, actually they are forced to do so, to shake the hands of these leaders, forced to smile and shout their support. Or they would report, despite evidence to the contrary, that these leaders were ignored by the people, that the people fear them. For the media and the Western governments, there is nothing right that these governments of the natives can do. And because they have convinced themselves through their own lies that these governments are bad, they would do their best do destabilise these countries. They would support and encourage anyone, NGOs in particular, to overthrow the government.

Some 50 years ago many of the colonies of the Western countries gained independence. But very quickly they realised that they had gained nothing of the sort. Economic pressure was used to deny independence for these countries. It was President Sukarno of Indonesia who first recognised this and called it “Neo-Colonialism”. He was laughed at by the world. But today economic pressure has replaced the gunboat to threaten independent countries. Just as in the colonial era, the regions of Asia, Africa and Latin America were unable to defend themselves, today the newly independent countries are unable to defend themselves.

They are terrified of being colonised once again through economic pressure coupled with the propaganda of the media. They are being terrorised; terrorised in the same way that the terrorists are threatening the world. Only economic terrorism is made out to be legitimate and to be deserving of support by everyone, including those of us in the developing countries.

If we are going to fend off this economic terrorism, we must first understand what is hitting us. Then we must work together within our own borders and between our countries. We are weak and we are client states, dependent on aid and loans. But still it is possible to take a common stand to fight off the threat. In this we will not be alone. There are forces within the rich countries themselves which are with us and we can enlist their help.

It is not that globalisation and the free market are bad. It is merely the interpretations of these ideas which are bad. If we come up with a proper interpretation, with proper safeguards for us, which recognise our weakness and our need for time, then globalisation and the free market can help us achieve economic growth and maintain our independence at the same time. It is entirely possible to do this. The debate must go on, and we will create a better world for ourselves and for the rich as well.

Economic terrorism must be defeated. The war against terrorism must be total and the end results must benefit everyone.

9

World in the midst of "World War III"

"Frightened, the world is taking measures to secure and defend at tremendous cost. But the main result is not security or freedom from terror attacks. The main result is to disrupt life, undermine investment and business, and generally to adversely affect economic growth worldwide."

IN the world today there is no trust or little trust, and governance, world governance, that is, is not good. We have, in fact, made a mess of the world. Two millennia of experience and mountains of

---

A speech delivered at the Plenary Session on "Trust and Governance for a New Era", organised by the World Economic Forum (WEF) in Davos, Switzerland, on January 23, 2003

knowledge have not made us much more capable at managing our affairs than Stone Age people.

We now live in fear, every one of us. We fear the terrorists. And the terrorists, their supporters or alleged supporters, fear us. We fear flying, we fear travelling to certain countries, we fear nightclubs, we fear letters, parcels and cargo containers, we fear white powder, shoes, Muslims, penknives, metal cutlery, etc. They, the other side, fear sanctions, starvation, shortage of medicine. They fear military invasion, being bombed and rocketed, being captured and detained.

People who are neutral, not involved, innocent—they too live in fear. They are the collaterals. Just as the Afghans and the Iraqi civilians are collaterals, the passengers on the hijacked planes and those people working in the World Trade Center towers are also collaterals.

Actually we are in the midst of "World War III", not the war against terrorists but the war between terrorists and the peace-loving anti-terrorists alliance, the war between the "axis of evil" and Satan. Both sides are convinced that they are right, that theirs is the fight against evil. Evil and Satan must be destroyed.

Frightened, the world is taking measures to secure and defend at tremendous cost. But the main result is not security or freedom from terror attacks. The main result is to disrupt life, undermine investment and business, and generally to adversely affect economic growth worldwide.

It is going to be a long war because hatred, anger and bitterness rule our hearts. We both want revenge. We both will retaliate. You kill our people, we will kill your people. And so it will go on and on. Sanity has deserted both sides.

The world has become small. It is said to be a Global Village. But we have not made much progress in the management of our world despite its diminished size. Just as in the Stone Age the man with the biggest club rules, in our modern and sophisticated Global Village the country with the biggest killing power rules.

When the Cold War ended we thought that the world would see peace and prosperity. After all, the people who believe in peace and universal justice won. The evil empire has been overthrown.

But the loss of a counterbalance has resulted in the great exponent of justice and fair play to become unbalanced. While the communists were there the capitalists curbed their greed and avarice. They showed a friendly face.

But now there is no more other side. The friendly face of capitalism is not needed any more. Capitalists now can do what they like and what they like is simply to make more money for themselves.

Why is there a need for borders? Why should countries protect their puny inefficient economies? The world has become too small to be divided into countries with different system of governments and laws. There should be just one global entity and one system, the great democratic system and the freedom that is supposed to go with it. If the new democracies do not know how to manage the system, that is too bad. Democracy is such a good system that everyone must adopt it. It is blasphemy to say anything against democracy. If you do, if you resist then you will be considered a heretic and starved to death, or bombed out of existence.

In a free world there must be competition. The strongest and the most efficient will win. If you are small, weak and inefficient, it is best that you go. In athletics it may be reasonable to have different classes of competitors. But in the competition between countries and corporations there should be no categorisation or classification, nor should handicaps be given. The biggest and the most efficient should be allowed to dominate and take all. It is good for everyone.

And so we see the great banks and corporations merging and acquiring each other to ensure that the tiny banks and businesses in the poor countries will not stand a chance and be swept aside.

Big is beautiful again. Big is good. Unfortunately, there is no guarantee that the big will not cheat, will not fall, will not go bankrupt. But we must not take notice of Enron, Global Crossing, Arthur Andersen, United Airlines, etc. They are the exceptions which merely prove the rule.

Today, the disparity between the rich and poor countries is greater than ever. The richest countries have a per-capita income of more than US$30,000, the poorest, US$300. Of the world's six billion people, one billion are underfed, underclothed and without a roof over their heads. Many scrounge in rubbish heaps for food, clothing and materials for their shelter.

In politics, the post-Cold War world is no better. The misfortunes of the weak are their problem. The strong will dominate.

Socially we have not advanced either. We talk a lot about the sanctity of human lives and human rights. We are opposed to death penalties. But actually whole populations have been sentenced to death and in many instances the sentence has been carried out. When war is declared against a country a death sentence is passed on the people and when war is executed the sentence is carried out. And still we talk glibly about the sanctity of life.

The exploitation of the world by the greedy, the double standards and the hypocrisy about human rights and respect for human lives, the oppression of the weak by the strong, the disregard for human suffering, the expropriation of other peoples' land and the expulsion of the people, all these have been aggravated by the ending of the Cold War and the victory of the righteous over the evil.

The worm finally turned. The weak have now hit back in the only way they can. Groping for the enemy, the strong hits out blindly in every direction, in every part of the world. No one is free. Fear rules the world.

With the onset of this "World War III", the world is in a state of turmoil. We now live in fear, even the rich are not as prosperous anymore, while the poor are actually poorer.

We have not made such a good job managing this Global Village of ours. There is no trust and no good governance.

So how do we create trust and good governance in the new era? I don't think it can be done by seeking a military defeat of the enemy and forcing them to submit. The forces against the "axis of evil" are not going to win because the target is wrong. All that can happen if they are defeated is to create more anger and a call for more revenge and retaliation by the people who are incensed by the injustice they believe they are experiencing.

On the other hand, the other side is not going to win either. The enemy is just too big and too powerful.

The only solution is through compromise. Trust must be built. The initiation must come from the good people. They must recognise that people do not tie bombs to their bodies or crash their planes for the fun of it. They must have a reason for it. We have to remove the reasons. Out-terrorising the terrorists will not work. But removing the causes of terrorism will.

Good governance is simple if we curb the greedy and forget about self-regulating markets. Governments are not yet anachronistic. They have a role to play.

We need a paradigm shift, we need a new mindset if we are ever going to put an end to this "World War III". We need victory for both, a victory where both sides will benefit.

The world is big and rich enough for everyone. There is no need to take everything for ourselves. A win-win solution is possible.

If we can overcome our anger and hatred, our craving for revenge, our unlimited greed, we can manage the world and achieve trust and eventually good governance.

10

Impact of terrorism on the world

"It is time we remove the causes. If we don't, if we continue to delude ourselves, then the fight against terrorists will never end and the change in the world caused by terrorism will remain permanent."

WHAT is obvious is that the fight against terrorism has already changed the world.

We were carefree before, criss-crossing the world in jet planes for pleasure and for business. The world had become a village, every part of it accessible in less than 24 hours from any other parts. Not only were the towns

---

A speech delivered at the World Economic Forum (WEF) in Davos, Switzerland, on January 24, 2003

almost identical in terms of buildings and facilities but we expected and we knew we could get the same food and drinks, hotels and shops and branded goods in every country across the world.

But we were not satisfied. We wanted identical political and economic systems, namely, democracy and deregulated free trade with identical laws and uniform practices as well. We wanted globalisation in a standard environment. Everyone must conform or be economically strangled.

We believe that there are far too many corporations in the world in each business. Most were financially weak and inefficient. We should get rid of all the small businesses and have only a few so-called super-giant multinational corporations to take over everything, from retailing noodles to producing and selling aeroplanes. Who needs papa-mama shops when hypermarkets can supply everything we need in life.

But there are countries which insist on protecting their little inefficient banks and industries. They must be eliminated. Sanctions should be applied. Markets should be closed to their products. And where they had somehow survived and developed their countries, undermine their currencies and destabilise them.

And so whole regions were made poor, forced to borrow from the rich, and become permanent debt slaves, completely compliant to the demand that they conform and accept globalisation.

It looked like things would go according to plan. The whole world was becoming a huge standard marketplace for the standard products and services of the consolidated, amalgamated, merged giant banks and corporations. There could only be greater growth and more wealth for the rich proponents of free trade and globalisation.

Yes, the poor would also benefit. They would provide cheap labour. Still automation and robots would throw most of them out of work. But that is the price we all have to pay for the technology which has made cheap and better products possible. The dole will take care of the unemployed. Too bad if the governments of the poor countries have no unemployment benefits. That is their problem. Free trade must be upheld at any cost.

Many people all over the world lived in abject poverty. And many live in fear of terror attacks. The Palestinians of course deserved to lose their country. For two long years the world watched in the comfort of their homes, 200,000 Bosnians being slaughtered. Bombs were periodically rained on Iraq, killing innocent civilians. In Northern Ireland, Protestants and Catholics live in fear of the next bomb. And in many parts of the world there were constant fears of terror attacks.

The world accepts that these people deserve what they got. They live in terror because they did not know how to protect themselves—to take security measures. Those who know and have the means would always be safe, watch terror from a safe distance.

Then literally out of the blue terror came to the wealthy and the protected. After September 11 no one is safe. And everyone anywhere can be the victims of terror attacks.

Unfortunately, having ignored terrorism as something that can only happen to others, the people most capable of tackling terrorism do not know how to tackle it. They can only think of improving their defenses with more stringent security measures and more sophisticated weapons. About 1.3 billion Muslims were identified as the potential enemy. They must be harassed, restrained and detained indiscriminately. Their shoes have to be examined. No penknives, paper cutters, metal cutlery on aircrafts. Every ship has to be thoroughly examined. Every port in the world must be checked constantly. Marshalls with weapons on every aircraft. And many, many more security measures.

All these have strained relations between many countries and people, affected economic development of the world adversely and domestic politics as well. Everyone is frightened of flying or travelling to certain countries, frightened of living at home, of investing, of receiving parcels, of large gatherings, of highrise buildings and parked vehicles. The tourist industry, the hospitality industry, the airlines have seen bankruptcies galore.

Against these enormous losses and the huge outlay on defence and security, the cost of mounting the attack such as on September 11 is minimal. No costly missiles. Just a dozen people in hijacked aircrafts can create havoc.

The question is, how long can all these defence or security measures be kept up? How long can we live in fear? How long can we withstand economic downturns? How long can the fight against terrorism be allowed to blight our life, to change the way we live?

So what should we do? The Israelis have the most thorough defence against terror attacks but the attacks are still going on. Abroad, the Israelis are sitting ducks. So are the other targets of the terrorists. Terrorising the terrorists as the Israelis have done has not reduced the number of terrorists. In fact, they seem to have increased. Attacking Iraq and getting rid of Saddam

Hussein is most likely to create more anger and increase the recruits for terror attacks.

For as long as there are people who are oppressed, whose land has been expropriated, whose sufferings have been ignored, for whom there is no justice, there will be terrorists and acts of terror. It only cost them their lives, something they seem to care very little about. The bombs can be made cheaply and the delivery vehicles hijacked.

Today, the whole world is suffused with hatred and anger. No one is seeking anything else except revenge. Both sides are saying "they will pay a heavy price for this".

Giving fancy reasons for the acts of terror will only result in our not taking the right actions. Is it true that Islam teaches its followers to terrorise non-Muslims? Is it true that Muslim poverty is at the root of their dastardly behaviour? Is it true that they envy the freedom and the democracy of the West?

September 11 was the work of people who were neither poverty-stricken, nor ignorant, nor even directly suffering from oppression. They were apparently ordinary people with families, sufficient income and enjoying a comfortable life. They were not Palestinians or Afghans or Libyans, Sudanese, Iraqis or Iranians, all of whom have good reasons to hate their Western detractors. Yet they were prepared to die a horrendous death. Given the opportunity, there will be others who will do it again.

It is time we examine the true causes of terrorism. It is time we remove the causes. If we don't, if we continue to delude ourselves, then the fight against terrorists will never end, and the change in the world caused by terrorism will remain permanent.

11

No longer just a war against terrorism

"... their acts [acts of terror] have also removed all the restraint in the countries of the north. They now no longer respect borders, international laws or even simple moral values. And they are now talking of wars, of the use of military conquests in order to change governments."

THE world now lives in fear. We are afraid of everything. We are afraid of flying, afraid of certain countries, afraid of bearded Asian men, afraid of the shoes airline passengers wear, of letters and parcels, of white powder. The countries allegedly harbouring terrorists, their people, innocent or otherwise, are

---

A speech delivered at the opening of the XIII Summit Meeting of the Non-Aligned Movement (NAM) in Kuala Lumpur, Malaysia, on February 24, 2003

afraid, too. They are afraid of war, of being killed, of being maimed by bombs dropped on them, by missiles fired from hundreds of miles away by unseen forces. They are afraid because they would become the collaterals to be killed because they get in the way of the destruction of their countries.

The preparations and the measures taken to ensure security go on frantically. Trillions of dollars are spent by the world on new weapons, new technology, new strategy, the deployment of forces and inspectors worldwide. Those who cannot afford these security measures must simply await their fate and trust in God. Yet despite all these, terror attacks have taken place where they are least expected, killing the collaterals again. There is still no guarantee that the well-dressed, clean-shaven family man next door might not become another hijacker, crashing his aircraft into buildings and killing collaterals.

In the meantime, the economy of the world has slowed down and in some instances has been reversed, with huge deficits burdening countries. Jobs are lost and poverty is increasing even in the rich countries. No new investments in foreign countries or at home. With the threat of war oil prices have shot up, increasing further the economic and social burdens of the poor countries.

Aid for the poor has practically stopped and loans are not available as the poor countries defaulted and defaulted again.

Truly the world is in a terrible mess, a state that is worse than during the East-West confrontation, the Cold War. All the great hopes following the end of the Cold War have vanished. And with the terrorists and the anti-terrorists fumbling blindly in their fight against each other, normalcy will not return for quite a long while.

Surely at some stage we must ask ourselves why this is happening to the world. Why is there terrorism? Is it true that the Muslims are born terrorists because of the teachings of a prophet who was a terrorist? How do we explain the pogroms, the inquisitions and the holocaust which characterised Christian Europe for almost 2000 years? Why did the Jews choose to seek haven in Muslim countries whenever Christian Europeans persecute them? Do people seek safety in the land of terrorists? Does not sound very likely.

The Christians, too, were terrorised, not by Muslims but by fellow Christians who condemned them as heretics. They were persecuted, tortured, burnt at the stakes for their beliefs and forced to migrate. Seems that the Muslims did not have a monopoly of terrorism, certainly not on the scale of the holocaust, the pogroms and the inquisition.

So it cannot be that Muslims are the sole cause of all these problems. If they are not, then is it a clash of civilisation, a clash of the Muslim civilisation against the Judeo-Christian civilisation, that is responsible.

Frankly, I do not think so. Frankly, I think it is because of a revival of the old European trait of wanting to dominate the world. And the expression of this trait invariably involves injustice and oppression of people of other ethnic origins and colours.

If we care to think back, there was no systematic campaign of terror outside Europe until the Europeans and the Jews created a Jewish state out of Palestinian land. Incidentally, terrorism was first used by the Haganah and the Irgun Zeva'i Le'umi to persuade the British to set up Israel. The Palestinians were actually ejected from their homes and their country and forced to live in miserable refugee camps for more than 50 years now.

It is the struggle of the Palestinians to regain their land that has precipitated, first conventional wars, then civil protests, and eventually violent demonstrations. The Israelis demanded European support to atone for European crimes against them in the past. In desperation the Palestinians finally resorted to what is described as acts of terror. Rightly, this is condemned by the world. But the world does not condemn as acts of terror the more terrifying acts of the Israelis: the massacres in Sabra and Shatila, the shooting and killing of children, the use of depleted uranium-coated bullets, the bulldozing of Palestinian homes while the occupants are still in them, the helicopter gunships, etc. And Israel is now threatening to use nuclear weapons.

This blatant double standards is what infuriates Muslims, infuriates them to the extent of launching their own terror attacks. If Iraq is linked to al-Qa'eda, is it not more logical to link the expropriation of Palestinian land and the persecution and oppression of Palestinians with September 11? It is not religious differences which angered the attackers of the World Trade Center. It is simply sympathy and anger over the expropriation of Palestinian land, over the injustice and the oppression of the Palestinians, and Muslims everywhere. If the innocent people who died in the attack on Afghanistan, and those who have been dying from lack of food and medical care in Iraq, are considered collaterals, are not the 3,000 who died in New York and the 200 in Bali also just collaterals whose deaths are necessary for the operations to succeed?

Actually the life of any human being is sacred, no matter if the person is a friend or an enemy. That is why war is not a solution. A contest based on who can kill more people in order to establish who the victor and who the loser is; worst still, in order to determine who is right and who is wrong is primitive and does not speak well of the so-called high level of civilisation we have achieved. The greatness of a nation should be based on a culture that values high moral qualities, aesthetics, learning and advancements in the sciences. Unfortunately, thousands of years after the Stone Age, we still measure the greatness of a nation by the capacity to slaughter the greatest number of people.

But the oppression and injustice is not confined to waging war and killing people; there is oppression in ideological propagation. We are now allowed only a democratic system of government. We admit it is by far the best system of government. But applying sanctions, starving people, denying access to medicine in order to force the acceptance of democracy hardly seem democratic. Actually millions have died because they have not converted to this new religion. And millions more are suffering because they are unable to make democracy work, because of the resulting anarchy.

Relieved of the need to compete with the communists, the capitalist free traders have ceased to show a friendly face. Their greed knows no bounds. They want countries which had fought hard to gain independence, to give up that independence, to do away with their borders, to allow the capitalists free access to do what they like to the economies of these countries. They call this free competition. As they merge and acquire each other, they become monstrous giants against whom the small businesses in the developing countries will not be able to compete. What is the meaning of competition if you cannot win at all. In the end a few of these monsters will control the economy of the whole world.

The sad thing is that they are not above cheating and corruption. And we know they can fail. We have seen how spectacularly they fail—losing US$100 billion in a year. And that is only one corporation.

Then there are the rogue currency traders who destroyed the economies of half the world, threw tens of millions out of work, bankrupted banks and thousands of businesses, cause the collapse of governments and precipitated anarchy; all so that half a dozen individuals can make billions for themselves.

Now the rich give no more aid. They do not lend either. And all the time the international agencies they control try to strangle the debt-laden poor countries which had been attacked by their greedy market manipulators.

The disparities between rich and poor widen daily. The rich have per-capita incomes of more than US$30,000, the poor only US$300. Still the rich want to squeeze out literally the last drop of blood from the poor.

It is this which plague the world today, this oppression of the poor by the rich; this injustice, this inequality. To rub salt into the wound the poor are always being told that they lack transparency and good governance, they don't respect human rights, they don't uphold freedom of speech, freedom of the press and so on and so forth, when, in fact, it is the rich who lack transparency, who do not respect human rights, who curb our rights to speak the truth about what they are doing, who use their media to hide their misdeeds and spread lies. How else can we interpret the operations of the hedge funds and the currency traders, sanctions and the systematic bombings of certain countries, the impoverishment of the already poor, and the censorship of news as well as distorted and fabricated reports about the south.

The fact is that the poor countries have been and are being oppressed and terrorised by the rich countries. Naturally the poor are bitter and angry and have lost faith in justice and honour. And the last straw which caused them to resort to futile and destructive terror attacks is the blatant support for state terrorism as practised by Israel and others. If Israeli terrorism is a response to Palestinian terrorism, then Palestinian terrorism and terror acts by their sympathisers must be due to the expulsion of Palestinians from their land, the further occupation of Palestinian territory and the open support for Israeli intransigence and terrorism by the Europeans. But the developing countries must admit that we are also responsible for the mess the world is in today. We have not used our independence and freedom to develop our countries for the good of our people. Instead we have been busy overthrowing our governments, setting up new governments which in turn would be overthrown. We have even killed our own people by the millions. And frequently, frustrated with anarchic democracy we resort to autocratic governments, exposing ourselves to much vilification.

The result of this confrontation between the haves and the have-nots, the developed and the developing, is a world that is practically ungovernable. Despite all the advances in science and technology, the world is in a terrible state. With more than enough food to feed the six billion or so people of the world, one in six is actually underfed, starving, with hundreds dying daily.

Since September 11, the rich and the powerful have become enraged with the poor half of the world. And their extreme measures to ensure security for themselves have only amplified the anger of the oppressed poor. Both sides are now in a state of blind anger and are bent on war, on killing each other.

War solves nothing. War is primitive. Today's war is more primitive than the wars fought during the Stone Age. The targets are not the fighters, the combatants. The target is the ordinary civilians, the women, the children and the aged. Whether it is terror attacks or military action, these are the victims.

In primitive wars, the carnage is witnessed by the warriors. While the suicidal terrorists die with each attack, the great warriors who press the buttons see nothing of the mangled bodies, the heads and limbs which are torn from disembowelled bodies, the blood and the gore of the innocent people who an instant before were living people like them. And because they don't see, the button-pressing warriors and the people who commanded them go back to enjoy a hearty meal, watch TV shows or moral-boosting troop entertainers and then retire to their cosy beds for a good night's sleep. Tomorrow they would make more sorties, to carpet bomb more children, women and old people or they would press more buttons to send missiles to tear off more heads and limbs.

War is about slaughtering people. Newer and more brutal weapons are being invented to kill more people more efficiently. And now there is talk that the use of nuclear weapons is justified. Is it because the people to be slaughtered are chromatically different? Is it because they cannot hit back?

Our meeting here today is a meeting of heads of states and heads of governments. We must admit that our organisation has not been as effective as it should be. We may want to remain uninvolved and to avoid incurring the displeasure of the powerful countries. But our people are getting restless. They want us to do something. If we don't, then they will, and they will go against us. They will take things into their own hands. Unable to mount a conventional war they will resort to guerrilla war, to terrorism, against us and against those they consider to be their oppressors.

They cannot be ignored any longer. We cannot incarcerate them all for we do not always know who they are or where they are.

September 11 has demonstrated to the world that acts of terror even by a dozen people can destabilise the whole world completely, put fear into the hearts of everyone, make them afraid of their own shadows.

But their acts have also removed all the restraint in the countries of the North. They now no longer respect borders, international laws or even simple moral values. And they are now talking of wars, of the use of military conquests in order to change governments. They are even talking of using nuclear weapons.

It is no longer just a war against terrorism. It is in fact a war to dominate the world, i.e., the chromatically different world. We are now being accused of harbouring terrorists, of being an "axis of evil", etc. NAM has a lot of problems and issues which it must tackle. But at the moment the most important threat that we face is the tendency of the powerful to wage war when faced with opposition to the spread of their dominance. We cannot fight a war with them.

Fortunately, many of their people are also sick of war. They have come out in their millions to protest the warlike policies of their leaders. We must join them. We must join their struggle with all the moral force that we can command.

War must be outlawed. That will have to be our struggle for now. We must struggle for justice and freedom from oppression, from economic hegemony. But we must remove the threat of war first. With this Sword of Damocles hanging over our heads we can never succeed in advancing the interests of our countries.

War must therefore be made illegal. The enforcement of this must be by multilateral forces under the control of the United Nations. No single nation should be allowed to police the world, least of all to decide what action to take, and when.

Globalisation must not be confined to the exploitation of the wealth of the earth only. Globalisation must include the multilateral protection of countries threatened by war or hegemony.

There must be a new world order in which power is shared equitably by all. The United Nations must be reformed. It must no longer be bound by the results of a world war fought more than half a century ago. Everyone must disarm. Weapons of mass destruction must be disallowed for all. And there should be no more research into making conventional weapons more lethal.

If it is right for an international agency in a globalised world to oversee human rights, business practices and the kind of democracy practised by countries, then a truly international agency beholden only to the United Nations General Assembly should oversee the military budget of all countries, both big and small. Trading in arms must come under the supervision of the United Nations. Brutal ethnic cleansing must be stopped by a multinational standing army.

When Japan was defeated, it was allowed to spend only one per cent of its GDP on its armed forces. If such a condition can be imposed on Japan, why not impose it on all countries?

In the struggle to outlaw war and control arms, nuclear as well as conventional, NAM will find growing support from among many people in the North. It is a daunting task nevertheless. But unless we take the moral high ground now, we will wait in vain for the powerful North to voluntarily give up slaughtering people in the name of national interest.

Again, I would like to say that NAM must struggle to outlaw war. It must struggle to outlaw nuclear weapons. It must struggle to stop the research and development of more and more lethal so-called conventional weapons. It must struggle to control the arms trade.

We must work for a new world order, where democracy is not confined to the internal governance of states only but to the governance of the world. We must work for the revival of the U.N. and multilateralism. We must work to do away or modify the powers of the victors of a war fought half a century ago.

We know we are weak. But we also know we have allies in the North. They too want the abolition of wars and the slaughtering of people for whatever reasons. They may not agree with us in everything. But in the opposition to war many will be with us. They are ready to oppose their warlike leaders. We must work with them.

This, then, is our struggle. We are not irrelevant. We are not anachronistic. We have a vision, the vision to build a new world order, a world order that is more equitable, more just, a world order which is, above all, free from the age-old belief that killing people is right, that it can solve the problems of relations between nations.

Glossary

ad-deen refers to the religion of Islam as a complete way of life, a whole system of thought and action: it includes all the connotations and significations associated with the faith, the beliefs, practices and teachings experienced and lived by Muslims individually and as a community

alim religious learned or scholar; theologian

fardu kifayah socially requisite knowledge; a Muslim's religious obligations to society

halal legitimate; permissible according to Muslim law and covering all aspects of life, usually pertaining to food

haram forbidden by Muslim law

hassanah bounty

imam leader of prayer in a congregation

Jahiliah pre-Islamic civilisation

kafir non-believer of Islam; infidel; pagan

khalifah caliph; in the past, a Muslim ruler; a title given to the acknowledged successors of Prophet Muhammad, regarded amongst Muslims as being vested with supreme dignity and power in all religious and civil-policy matters

mazhab school of Islam thought

Quran the Holy Book of Islam

shahid martyr

ulama plural of *alim*, which means 'learned' or 'scholar'; Islamic scholars or those learned in Islam; seekers of knowledge; theologians. Though, traditionally, *ulama* have claimed the right to interpret Islam, the modern period has seen an erosion of their traditional powers and authority. Most of them continue to maintain that they alone possess the requisite religious learning and thus ought to be the ultimate authority to determine what the law should be.

ummah the worldwide community comprising all adherents of the Islamic religion; the *ummah* is a supranational notion that extends beyond national boundaries and political borders to encompass all Muslims, regardless of political affiliations

warasah the successor (of the Prophet)

zakat a religious obligation requiring Muslims with economic or financial means to contribute a certain percentage of their wealth as alms and tithes, *zakat* (an Islamic property tax) and *fitrah* (a special tithe during the festival of *Aidil Fitri*). Alms are used to help the poor, widows and orphans, and assist in the spread of the religion. The payment of *zakat* is a formal duty, not subject to choice, and is not charity; it is an act of worship or thanksgiving to God and of service to the community. In this way, society is not faced with the problem of excessive imbalance.

Index

Dr Mahathir Mohamad has been prime minister of Malaysia since July 16, 1981. One of the most durable and outspoken figures on the world political stage, he first came to prominence in 1969 when he was expelled from the ruling party, UMNO, for writing a letter critical of the then-prime minister, Tunku Abdul Rahman. Before being readmitted to UMNO in 1972, he wrote his famous, highly controversial work, *The Malay Dilemma*(1970), which examined the economic backwardness of the Malays, and advocated state intervention to bring about their rehabilitation. The book was promptly banned in Malaysia. In *The Challenge* (1986), he explodes fallacies and exposes distortions concerning religion, education, democracy, communism, freedom and discipline, and the concerns of this world and the next. In *A New Deal for Asia*(1999), Dr Mahathir reflects on Malaysia's fight for independence and rails against those who blindly worship the free market.

As Malaysia's fourth prime minister, Dr Mahathir has played a pivotal role in the confident march of his people towards Vision 2020, his blueprint for Malaysia's advance towards fully developed status. Born on December 20, 1925, Dr Mahathir studied medicine in Singapore, where he met his future wife, Dr Siti Hasmah Mohd Ali. After working as a doctor in government service, he left to set up his own private medical practice in his hometown, Alor Setar. In 1974, he gave that up to concentrate on his political career. Dr Mahathir and his wife have seven children and ten grandchildren.